STERLING BIOGRAPHIES

LOU GEHRIG

Iron Horse of Baseball

James Buckley, Jr.

STERLING

New York / London
www.sterlingpublishing.com/kids

I'd like to thank all the athletes who, like Lou Gehrig, combine outstanding physical gifts with generosity of spirit and enthusiasm for life.

This biography of Lou Gehrig was built on the shoulders of giants. From the great Paul Gallico to Eleanor Gehrig, and from more recent writers such as Ray Robinson and Jonathan Eig, many fine writers and scholars have done a lot of legwork on the Gehrig life and legend. I hope I've added my own touches of interest or points of emphasis, but without the work of these writers and others, this book would be a shell of its current state. I thank them for their scholarship and inspiration.

STERLING and the distinctive Sterling logo are registered trademarks of Sterling Publishing Co., Inc.

Library of Congress Cataloging-in-Publication Data
Buckley, James, 1963–
   Lou Gehrig : Iron Horse of baseball / by James Buckley, Jr.
      p. cm. — (Sterling biographies)
   Includes bibliographical references and index.
   ISBN 978-1-4027-7151-4 (hardcover) — ISBN 978-1-4027-6363-2 (pbk.) 1. Gehrig, Lou, 1903–1941—Juvenile literature. 2. Baseball players—United States—Biography—Juvenile literature. 3. New York Yankees (Baseball team)—Juvenile literature. I. Title.
   GV865.G4B835 2010
   796.357092—dc22
   [B]
                                                                                        2009024236

Lot #: 10   9   8   7   6   5   4   3   2   1
12/09

Published by Sterling Publishing Co., Inc.
387 Park Avenue South, New York, NY 10016
© 2010 by James Buckley, Jr.

Distributed in Canada by Sterling Publishing
c/o Canadian Manda Group, 165 Dufferin Street
Toronto, Ontario, Canada M6K 3H6
Distributed in the United Kingdom by GMC Distribution Services
Castle Place, 166 High Street, Lewes, East Sussex, England BN7 1XU
Distributed in Australia by Capricorn Link (Australia) Pty. Ltd.
P.O. Box 704, Windsor, NSW 2756, Australia

Printed in China
All rights reserved

Sterling ISBN 978-1-4027-7151-4 (hardcover)
             ISBN 978-1-4027-6363-2 (paperback)

Image research by James Buckley, Jr., and Jim Gigliotti

For information about custom editions, special sales, premium and corporate purchases, please contact Sterling Special Sales Department at 800-805-5489 or specialsales@sterlingpublishing.com.

Contents

Events in the Life of Lou Gehrig

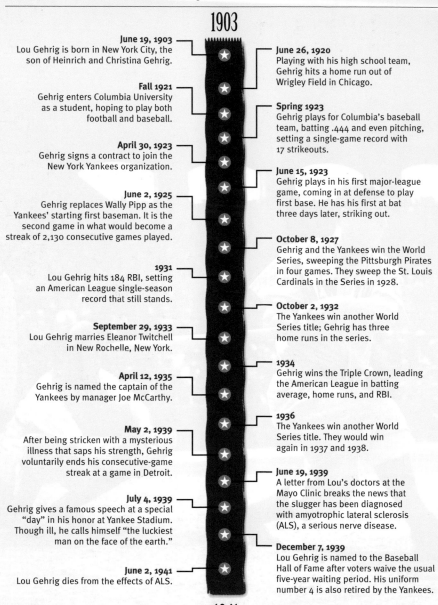

1903

June 19, 1903
Lou Gehrig is born in New York City, the son of Heinrich and Christina Gehrig.

Fall 1921
Gehrig enters Columbia University as a student, hoping to play both football and baseball.

April 30, 1923
Gehrig signs a contract to join the New York Yankees organization.

June 2, 1925
Gehrig replaces Wally Pipp as the Yankees' starting first baseman. It is the second game in what would become a streak of 2,130 consecutive games played.

1931
Lou Gehrig hits 184 RBI, setting an American League single-season record that still stands.

September 29, 1933
Lou Gehrig marries Eleanor Twitchell in New Rochelle, New York.

April 12, 1935
Gehrig is named the captain of the Yankees by manager Joe McCarthy.

May 2, 1939
After being stricken with a mysterious illness that saps his strength, Gehrig voluntarily ends his consecutive-game streak at a game in Detroit.

July 4, 1939
Gehrig gives a famous speech at a special "day" in his honor at Yankee Stadium. Though ill, he calls himself "the luckiest man on the face of the earth."

June 2, 1941
Lou Gehrig dies from the effects of ALS.

June 26, 1920
Playing with his high school team, Gehrig hits a home run out of Wrigley Field in Chicago.

Spring 1923
Gehrig plays for Columbia's baseball team, batting .444 and even pitching, setting a single-game record with 17 strikeouts.

June 15, 1923
Gehrig plays in his first major-league game, coming in at defense to play first base. He has his first at bat three days later, striking out.

October 8, 1927
Gehrig and the Yankees win the World Series, sweeping the Pittsburgh Pirates in four games. They sweep the St. Louis Cardinals in the Series in 1928.

October 2, 1932
The Yankees win another World Series title; Gehrig has three home runs in the series.

1934
Gehrig wins the Triple Crown, leading the American League in batting average, home runs, and RBI.

1936
The Yankees win another World Series title. They would win again in 1937 and 1938.

June 19, 1939
A letter from Lou's doctors at the Mayo Clinic breaks the news that the slugger has been diagnosed with amyotrophic lateral sclerosis (ALS), a serious nerve disease.

December 7, 1939
Lou Gehrig is named to the Baseball Hall of Fame after voters waive the usual five-year waiting period. His uniform number 4 is also retired by the Yankees.

1941

O, Lucky Man

Today, I consider myself the luckiest man on the face of the earth.

On July 4, 1939, Lou Gehrig stepped to home plate at Yankee Stadium. He'd been doing that regularly since 1925. In fact, until a few weeks earlier, he had not missed a single game with the Yankees—he played 2,130 in a row. He had also done very well at that plate, putting up Hall-of-Fame statistics, including an incredible number of home runs and **runs batted in (RBI)** season after season. He had also helped his team win six World Series.

However, what made Gehrig's appearance on July 4 different from all the others was that the soft-spoken, humble hero used a microphone instead of a bat. It was Lou Gehrig Appreciation Day, and tens of thousands waited in silence for him to speak. Gehrig had been forced from the lineup by illness just two months earlier, an illness that looked like it would end his career.

Most men would have been bitter at such a turn of events. Many would have been angry. Gehrig, however, showed that had as much courage as he had batting skill. In the face of this sad news, he came through with another home run when he said, "Today, I consider myself the luckiest man on the face of the earth."

CHAPTER 1

A Good German Family

He's the only egg in my basket . . . so I want him to have the best.

    —Christina Gehrig

In the late 1800s, **immigrants** from across Europe were pouring into the United States. Of those that came from Germany, many moved to a part of New York City called Yorkville, on the east side of Manhattan island. Some people called 86th Street, which ran through the neighborhood, Sauerkraut Avenue after a popular German dish. That's where Heinrich and Christina Gehrig found themselves after arriving from Germany—Heinrich in 1887 and Christina in 1900. That's where their son Heinrich Ludwig (Henry Louis) Gehrig was born on June 19, 1903. He was known by his middle name, and was usually called Lou.

The Gehrigs had three other children—daughters Anna, born in 1902, and Sophie, 1904, and another boy who did not live long enough to name—but, sadly, none of them lived very long. Lou Gehrig had not yet been born when his sister Anna died, and his sister Sophie lived for only a year and a half. Money was often tight for the Gehrig's, but even if they could have afforded it, medicine was not nearly as good then as it is today. Childhood diseases were much harder to treat back then, and it was common for parents to lose their young ones, as the Gehrig family's sad tale shows. Only Lou, solid and strong, survived. As the only child in the family, he received all of his mother's attention—something that would be true throughout his life. "He's the only egg in my basket . . . so I want him to have the best," Christina said. Lou returned her affection and attention, even as a grown man.

Lou and His Mom

Christina was the most important person to Lou throughout his life. As he moved through school, baseball, and career, she was always at the center. He wanted her approval, he bowed to her wishes; he (for the most part) did whatever she said.

Part of the reason was that, as noted, he was an only child. Without siblings to play with, Lou devoted his attention to his mother. Similarly, with only one child to raise, Christina was able to focus fully on him. Christina was obsessed with making sure that Lou grew healthy and strong, piling plates of food in front of him at every meal. She made him focus on his studies, which he didn't always enjoy. She would eventually make him go to high school and college at a time when many young men went right to work after grade school.

Christina was a powerful woman, both in personality and physical presence, having nearly two hundred pounds on her short, stocky frame. Add to that her dedicated mission to make "Looie" as good as he could be, and it was not surprising that she commanded such attention from her son.

Lou's early years were spent amid the heavily German neighborhood of Yorkville. He spoke German with his parents and would often do so throughout his life. Their shared language was another bond between Lou and Christina. Even when Lou became a big baseball star, he was still her German-speaking little boy.

In Gehrig's Yorkville neighborhood, signs in German, such as at this movie theater, were not uncommon.

As a kid, Lou was shy and did not make friends easily. His shyness and his clumsiness at games—at first—led to teasing from neighborhood kids. This was another thing that made him cling ever more tightly to his mother, for whom he could do no wrong. Meanwhile, Christina had to work several jobs, including cooking at people's homes and taking in laundry. She gave Lou a few pennies to deliver the clean laundry. Seeing up close how hard she worked to help support the family made Gehrig feel even more connected to her. It was a bond that would become the strongest in his life.

The Sporting Life

As he was growing up, Lou loved games, sports, and activity. He enjoyed going to watch the New York Giants, the National League baseball team that played in Manhattan, not far from the Gehrigs' home. He collected baseball cards that came in the packages of cigarettes his father smoked.

The combination of his mother's heavy cooking and visits with his father to German gyms known as *turnvereins* meant that Lou became tall and strong. As an adult, Lou often told a story that illustrated his physical endurance as a child: Sick with a fever, Lou was told to stay in bed and miss school. However, as soon as his mother left for work, he climbed out of bed and went to class. In his school days, he was an "iron man," calling to mind even then the nickname that he would later earn as a baseball player—the Iron Horse.

JOSS, CLEVELAND

This 1908 Addie Joss card is an example of the type of baseball card young Lou collected.

Turnvereins

In the years that Lou was growing up in New York City, it was unusual for people to work out, as many people do today. People almost never went to gyms, jogged, or lifted weights. One exception was a popular pastime among the Gehrigs' German-American neighbors. They spent hours at places called *turnvereins*, which were traditional German gyms. These gyms were named for Friedrich Ludwig Jahn, who was often called Turnvater Jahn, or Father of Gymnastics Jahn. Men young and old—and even some women and girls—would practice gymnastics, jump rope, swing wooden clubs, and toss medicine balls, which are heavy, leather bags. Lou went first with his father and then by himself. In a time when even great athletes were not typically as muscular as they are today, the body that Gehrig developed, partly thanks to turnvereins, stood out in a crowd.

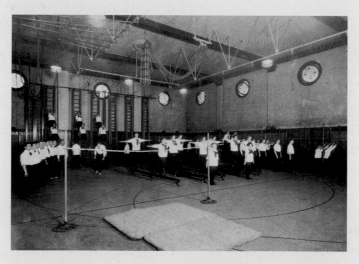

Gymnastics was one of the popular activities at turnvereins, as shown here.

A Move Uptown

In 1908, when Lou was five, the Gehrigs left the German haven of Yorkville for an area of Manhattan called Washington Heights. It was still far from luxurious, and it was a neighborhood of people from mixed backgrounds. Lou was no longer amid the comfortable surroundings of a mostly German neighborhood. Now at PS (Public School) 132, he was tossed into the ethnic swirl that included Irish, Italian, and other nationalities. His shyness became a problem again as his classmates, often quick to pester a newcomer, found every excuse to tease him. They called him chicken heart, and often wouldn't let him play in their schoolyard games. In fact, according to famous sports writer Paul Gallico, who wrote a book about Gehrig in 1941, Gehrig was "an undistinguished [player] on the PS 132 ball team, a left-handed catcher who couldn't hit, a chicken heart who was so ball shy he [could barely reach the plate.]" However, Gehrig loved to play baseball, and he did everything he could to be included in the games. He had his mother's determination to succeed, and he never stopped trying to improve his skills.

Gehrig was also teased about his clothing, for both its quality and fit. He often wore second-hand clothes that didn't quite fit him. He started a habit then that he would carry into adulthood: almost never wearing an overcoat or winter clothing. In the coldest New York winters, he would go to school in khaki pants, a button-down shirt, and boots.

. . . Gehrig loved to play baseball, and he did everything he could to be included in the games.

Throughout these years, young Lou continued to be shy and seemed to lack confidence. As great as he would someday be in sports and in the public eye, he seemed to some to always remain that shy and withdrawn boy. He didn't make many friends, spent most of his time at home (when not playing ball), and seemed to be "worried" a lot.

Eventually, though, he found a few pals to hang around with, and they found things to do . . . and trouble to get into. He and his friends would often swim in the Hudson River, just to the west of their homes in Washington Heights. One time, Gehrig managed to swim all the way to Fort Lee, on the New Jersey side of the river. Another time, he and a friend were arrested by a police officer for swimming without trunks. Lou's father had to pick him up at the police station, and, not surprisingly, was not pleased with his son's behavior. Still, this was a rare moment of trouble for Gehrig. He was a good German

Gehrig and his pals cooled off in New York's rivers like the boys in this photograph.

boy, and German boys did what their mothers and fathers told them to do.

However, by 1914, when Lou was eleven, being German suddenly added to his problems. In Europe, German armed forces were battling several European countries in what would become World War I. The United States would not enter the war until 1917, but from its early days, the war generated bad feelings about German people in the United States. Gehrig endured taunts and teasing. Kids called him "Krauthead" and "Heinie" and other names meant to make fun of his background.

Gehrig posed for this graduation picture after finishing his studies at PS 132 in 1917.

German Americans and the War

In 1914, World War I began in Europe. The forces of Germany were battling those of England, France, and other allies of America. In 1917, the United States entered the war, and life became very uncomfortable for the Gehrigs and other Germans living in America. They were suddenly viewed with suspicion, as being "the enemy." Some people called for them to be arrested, sent home to Germany, or at least investigated. Some used violence against these immigrants. Even **major league** baseball was affected, as some players of German background changed their names to hide their ethnicity. For example, the Cincinnati Reds star "Heinie" Groh reverted to his given name of Henry, because Heinie was a nickname given to many Germans. When the war ended, the feelings and problems slowly disappeared.

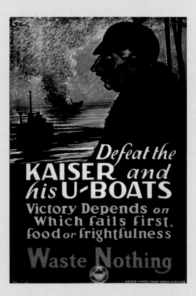

World War I posters such as this one helped fuel anti-German feelings among Americans.

CHAPTER 2

A Budding Star

When I got there and saw so many people going into the field and heard all the cheering and noise, I was so scared I couldn't see straight.

Christina Gehrig once again got her way after Lou completed his studies at PS 132. While his classmates took jobs in butcher shops or in warehouses or factories, Lou went to high school. Christina chose Commerce High School, which was actually several miles away from their home, because of its focus on engineering and math. Beginning in 1917, Lou had to take an elevated train every day back and forth the 100 or so blocks between home and school.

Christina was determined that Lou would stick to his studies, but Lou continued to feel the pull of the sports field. He was not yet the well-coordinated athlete he would soon become, but he loved the action of the games. On the sports field, Gehrig didn't have to worry about his shyness, his family's money problems, or his schoolwork. He could just run and play. He took part in youth leagues away from the school grounds, much as kids today play in Little League or Pony League.

For his first year in high school, however, Lou didn't play on any of Commerce's teams. Some accounts say that it was solely to please Christina that he didn't try out for any sports. At one time, he was quoted as saying,

Gehrig is sitting at the front right of this photo of one of his schoolboy teams.

"I wanted to play ball on the school team but lacked the courage to try out for a position."

A story about how he was convinced to play on the Commerce baseball team is more evidence of his shyness. After some of the other kids at school told a teacher and a coach about their big friend's hitting ability in the youth leagues, the teacher ordered him to come to a game. "I went up to the stadium on a streetcar. When I got there and saw so many people going into the field and heard all the cheering and noise, I was so scared I couldn't see straight. I turned right around and got back on the streetcar and went home. The next day, the teacher threatened to flunk me if I didn't show up for the next game."

Even as his baseball skills continued to improve, and as close as Lou and his mother were, Mrs. Gehrig didn't understand

Shown here is an example of some of the type of gear Gehrig and his friends might have used. Compared to the large baskets of baseball gloves used by today's players, this mitt is quite small.

her son's love of sports in general, and baseball, in particular. "This baseball is a waste of time. It will never get you anywhere," she said. For his part, Mr. Gehrig wasn't much more aware of the game, but in an effort to show his support, he once gave Lou a catcher's mitt as a gift. One problem: It was for a right-handed player—Mr. Gehrig's son was a lefty.

When Lou finally did start playing sports for Commerce, he discovered that his days on the schoolyard, swimming in the Hudson, and working hard with his mother at her jobs and with his father at the gyms had given him strength and endurance. He started out in football in the fall, in which he soon became a bone-rattling tackler. He played soccer, which had been popular in his old Yorkville neighborhood. Oddly, baseball was probably his weakest sport.

Though Gehrig played first base and pitched, he was not very successful as an outfielder. However, he was strong—much stronger than other boys his age—and he could hit a baseball farther than many big leaguers could. He showed his ability to work hard, too. Baseball coach Harry Kane spent extra time with the young player. Kane, who played for a short time in the major leagues before becoming a coach at Commerce, recognized that Gehrig had trouble hitting curveballs. These tricky pitches change direction on their way to home plate. Even older, more experienced hitters have trouble with them. In Gehrig's case, he hit left-handed. Curveballs from left-handed pitchers gave him the most trouble of all. Kane set about to fix that and threw curve after curve for Gehrig to hit.

"We set to work together and after a few weeks of practice, day in and day out, he completely overcame his fault," Kane remembered.

High School Star

By the time Lou was a junior, he had developed into a powerfully built athlete. He stood six feet tall and weighed 180 solid pounds. He excelled at football, using his size and strength to play several positions. It was at baseball, however, that he became the most outstanding. His hours of hard work with the coach, along with his strength and blossoming athletic ability, had turned Lou into the best hitter in New York high school baseball. With Lou as its slugging star, the Commerce baseball team had become the top high school team in New York City. Hundreds of people attended their games, and local newspapers regularly wrote stories about the team and its players. It was a new feeling for Lou, to be talked about and spotlighted like this. He was uncomfortable with the attention, of course, being such a shy person. Once he stepped onto the field, though, his shyness disappeared and he played his best. He might not have admitted it out loud, but Gehrig was becoming a star. In fact, some of the newspaper stories about him and his hitting feats called Lou the "Babe Ruth of high school baseball." Ruth was the star of the New York Yankees at the time, and the most powerful slugger in baseball history. To compare a big, strapping seventeen-year-old to the mighty Ruth was very special indeed.

HIGH SCHOOL OF COMMERCE
1920 NATIONAL HIGH SCHOOL BASEBALL CHAMPIONS

In this photo of the 1920 Commerce High team that traveled to Chicago, Gehrig is seated third from the right in the second row.

In June 1920, as part of a special event put on by a New York newspaper, the impressive Commerce High baseball team was invited to travel to Chicago to play another great high school team, Lane Technical. The newspaper paid all the Commerce team's expenses. Lou was excited to make the trip, but he had one person to convince: his mother.

Christina was afraid that the five-day excursion would interrupt his studies. She still didn't understand his attraction to baseball. She had expectations that he would be an engineer or an architect, not a ballplayer. After much pleading, Lou got her to agree to the journey. He and his teammates left on a train to Chicago, the first time most of them had ever left New York City.

As a sign of just how big the team was in the eyes of its fans, more than 8,000 people packed into Grand Central Station to see the Commerce team start its trip.

In Chicago

The journey itself was a big deal, let alone the chance to play against Lane in Cubs Park, as the home of the National League's Chicago Cubs was known then. On the long ride there, the players ate in the fancy railroad dining car on tablecloths and with nice silverware. They watched as the fields and towns of the upper Midwest rolled by. In addition, they were surprised to find themselves treated as celebrities of a sort. People traveling on the train wanted to meet the young stars that had earned a trip to Chicago to play baseball. One visitor was William Howard Taft, the former president of the United States, also on his way to Chicago. He was introduced to all the players and reportedly said, "I look forward to seeing you boys play." It was a memorable moment for Lou and all the young men. Of course, for Lou, the future major-league star, this was just the first of many times that baseball would send him on a train ride.

One visitor was William Howard Taft, the former president of the United States, also on his way to Chicago.

In Chicago, the players went first to Comiskey Park where they saw the American League's (A.L.'s) Chicago White Sox beat the Cleveland Indians 6–3. After staying overnight in a hotel—another first for most of the boys—they went to Cubs Park for their big game. Though Lou came in with a reputation as a slugger, he didn't show much during his first few at bats, making outs in two of three trips to

Cubs Park was renamed Wrigley Field in 1926 to honor the club's owner at the time, William Wrigley, Jr. The Chicago ballpark remains one of the great baseball palaces in the country.

the plate. In the ninth inning, though, he got one more chance. The score was Commerce 8, Lane 6, and with the bases loaded (runners on all three bases) and two outs for his team, the pressure was on Lou. However, as with many of baseball's greats, Lou thrived under this stress. He crushed the first pitch he saw. The ball flew away, high and far, above the right-field bleachers and completely out of the ballpark—a **grand slam**! The runners on the bases and Lou all sprinted to home plate, bringing Commerce's score up to 12. "Gehrig's blow would have made any big leaguer proud, yet it was walloped by a boy who hadn't even started to shave," read an article in the *Chicago Tribune*.

The train ride home was just as much fun as the ride to Chicago. This time, it was a victory party. The team was met at Grand Central Station in New York by a cheering crowd of parents, students, and neighbors, welcoming back the heroes. After seeing his name in the Chicago papers after the game, Gehrig returned to New York to find his name all over his hometown newspapers, too, especially the *Daily News*, which had sponsored the team on its trip. Baseball—though Mrs. Gehrig still wasn't sure about it—was taking her son places whether she liked it or not.

Not only did Gehrig play for Commerce teams, he also played for **semipro** baseball teams during the summertime, frequently pitching against grown men. Companies often organized these teams for their employees to play on and to advertise their company's products. The players all had other jobs and were not full-time ballplayers. When Gehrig was sixteen, he played for a team organized by the Otis Elevator Company. He was paid a few dollars for some of these games, which was one thing about baseball that his mother didn't object to.

Gehrig wasn't done with high school sports, however. The following fall, as a senior, he starred for Commerce's football team, especially in a big game against DeWitt Clinton High. Although Commerce lost, Gehrig's talent shone through. After the game, he met Bobby Watt, the manager for Columbia University's sports teams. Located in upper Manhattan, Columbia was not far from the Gehrigs' home. Watt wanted Gehrig to attend Columbia (although the young man would have to take some additional classes to qualify for the school). Watt wanted Gehrig on his baseball team.

The Gehrigs knew the college well. While Lou was in high school, his father, Heinrich, had become very sick and couldn't

The Low Memorial Library at Columbia University, pictured here, is the most prominent building on the University's main campus in the Morningside Heights neighborhood of New York City.

work for a long time. He was a metalworker, and his illness kept him at home for many days. Some **biographers** have blamed his illness on drinking or speculated that he was lazy. Still others blame a combination of the two. Whatever the cause, the result was that Mrs. Gehrig began taking on more jobs. One was as a cook at a **fraternity** called Sigma Nu (fraternities are named with letters from the Greek alphabet) at Columbia University.

Lou decided to take Watt up on his offer and join his mother on campus. Lou Gehrig, future baseball star, became a college man.

CHAPTER 3

Columbia and the Pros

Here is a kid who can't miss.
    —Yankees' scout Paul Krichell

Before Gehrig could enter Columbia University, however, he had to earn additional credits. He had not been a strong student in high school, so he had to take more classes to qualify for college. Although he graduated high school in January, he later spent months taking courses at a summer school in subjects he had not covered at Commerce. Even though he was not yet officially a student, he was allowed to practice with the Columbia baseball team, and he made a great first impression, whacking a pair of home runs (commonly called homers) in an exhibition game.

Columbia's student newspaper reporter must not have been at that game—or read all the reports about Gehrig's success in high school—because the reporter certainly

Though Lou was not permitted to play baseball during his first year as a college student, he eventually joined the team. This photograph shows Gehrig in his Columbia University uniform.

underestimated the school's new ballplayer. "Gehrig, our first sacker, can certainly field, but he is woefully weak at the bat," the paper reported.

Before Gehrig finally entered Columbia, he had a brush with pro baseball. In the spring of 1921, he tried out for the New York Giants after a scout saw how good the young man could be. Scouts are employees of big-league teams that search for young talent. They watch high school and college games, trying to find players to fill their organizations' **rosters**.

The great Giants' manager John McGraw missed a chance to add Gehrig to his talented team.

Gehrig traveled uptown to the Polo Grounds, home to the great National League team, to meet its famous manager, John McGraw. Though known as an excellent judge of talent, McGraw, like the Columbia newspaper, missed the boat on this one. After watching Gehrig hit a few balls, McGraw sent him out to field some ground balls. There, he saw him boot, or miss, an easy grounder, botching what should have been a simple play. "That's it, get that guy out of here, I've got enough lousy players," shouted McGraw. The Giants' connection did, however, lead to the first and only scandal of Gehrig's life.

A Season Without Sports

In those days, and for the most part in these days as well, it was against the rules for college players to accept money

In a posed photo typical of the time, Gehrig shows how he would stretch to catch a low throw at first base.

for playing a sport. Gehrig made a mistake in the summer of 1921 when he played a few games for a **minor-league** team in Hartford, Connecticut. (McGraw didn't want Gehrig for the Giants, but his scouts found a spot for Gehrig with their lower, minor-league team.) Gehrig probably had some idea that what he was doing was wrong, though, as he played under a false name, "Lou Lewis." In any case, he played for two weeks. He had a .261 **batting average** and earned his first serious money playing baseball. However, those two weeks would turn out to cost him a lot in other ways.

His Columbia baseball coach, Andy Coakley, found out about Gehrig's "summer job" and told him to stop right away. He knew that his future star might not be allowed to play college sports if he had already played professionally (his teenage semipro games didn't really count against him in this case). The damage was done, however. Having broken the rules, Gehrig was told he could not play sports for Columbia during the 1921–1922 school year.

On the bright side, this situation thrilled his mother, who could watch her son from her post in the kitchen as he became a full-time college student.

Lou took a full range of classes, including English literature, civilization, mathematics, and German. Oddly, although he still spoke German with both of his parents, he flunked that course. It's one thing to speak a language, it's another to be able to read and write it. However, as he did in sports, Lou worked hard, put in the time, and made it through his freshman year.

Columbia Lou

When Gehrig's suspension from sports was lifted for his second year, he made the most of it. He was an instant star on the football team, playing offense and defense. Columbia's team wasn't very good, but Gehrig was among the team's best players. He saw time as a **running back**, scoring several touchdowns, and as a **punter**. He also played line on defense,

Gehrig was a star with the Columbia football team, too.

using his six-foot, 180-pound body to make sure and solid tackles. As well as he played in football, however, he was just waiting for baseball season to start in March.

Once baseball began, Gehrig got off to a fast start, clubbing homer after homer. Columbia legend says that one of his mighty blasts broke a window in the school library; but in reality, that building was too far even for Gehrig to reach. He did hit a sundial located about 450 feet from home plate. By April, he was one of the team's top all-around players, pitching at many games. On April 18, 1923, Lou had his finest game as a college student, striking out a school-record seventeen batters in Columbia's loss to Williams College. On the same day, across the river in the Bronx, the brand-new Yankee Stadium was opening to the public. Babe Ruth hit a homer as the New York Yankees beat the Boston Red Sox 4–1. Lou didn't know it at the time, but he would be playing at Yankee Stadium in just a few short months.

Gehrig ended that season at Columbia with a batting average of .444. With .300 the average for a very good hitter, that mark showed just how much better he was than his competition. Gehrig's success at Columbia drew the scouts from the major leagues. The major-league teams are at the top of a pyramid of teams. Below them are several levels of minor-league teams. The best players work their way up from high school and college through the minors to reach the majors. Not many make that long trip, but it is the scouts' job to find players who are good enough to try.

Oddly, however, the scout who would change Gehrig's life didn't show up specifically to watch him. Yankees scout Paul Krichell was attending a Columbia game at Rutgers, a university in New Jersey, as part of his regular route of local schools.

Baseball in 1923

Today, Major League baseball boasts thirty teams, located across the country and even in Canada. Millions of fans fill the ballparks, and every game can be seen on television. There are three rounds of playoffs before the World Series. In 1923, however, the National and American Leagues had only eight teams each. Chicago and St. Louis had teams, but that was as far west as the major leagues went. There were no playoffs, and the league champions went right to the World Series. Players made far, far less money. The average player earned about $8,000—about $85,000 by today's standards. Compare that to the average salary in 2008 of $3.1 million. Because they were only paid during the season, players in those early days often had to find other jobs in the off-season, and only a select few earned enough to have baseball as their only job.

Yankee Stadium, pictured here, opened on April 18, 1923, and set a new standard for baseball stadiums. It closed in 2008 and a new, larger, even more grand and upgraded Yankee Stadium opened next door in 2009.

"I didn't go there to look at Gehrig, actually. I didn't even know what position he played. But he played outfield against Rutgers and socked a couple of balls a mile. I sat up and took notice. I saw a tremendous youth, with powerful arms and terrific legs. I said, 'Here is a kid who can't miss.'"

Krichell, according to some legends, called Gehrig "the next Babe Ruth," a possible early connection to the man with whom Lou would be linked throughout his career. Whether that is true or not, Krichell knew he had a hot prospect. Krichell convinced the Yankees general manager, Ed Barrow, that Gehrig would be perfect for the organization. He invited Gehrig to the new Yankee Stadium to meet Barrow and sign a contract. The Yankees offered to pay Gehrig a salary for the rest of the 1923 season, plus give him a bonus of $1,500. In those days, that was enough money to lift the entire Gehrig family out of poverty for good.

However, Gehrig did pause to consider the offer. He spoke with a Columbia business professor, who told him that, judging by how Gehrig had done in his class, the young man had better stick to baseball. For his part, Gehrig knew what it meant to leave school and how it would affect his mother. "The money they put before me was enough to turn any kid's head. I still was not sure I wanted to go into baseball as a steady profession [job], but I decided to grab what I could of it." Mrs. Gehrig (and Lou in the off-season) would still have to work, but they wouldn't have to worry about not having money again. It was not her first choice for her son, but the money was something Christina could not ignore. Besides, she probably thought, he could always get a better job in the winter when he was not playing baseball.

> "I sat up and took notice. I saw a tremendous youth, with powerful arms and terrific legs."

Ed Barrow (1868–1953)

The man who signed Lou Gehrig to his first baseball contract was one of the most talented executives in baseball history. Ed Barrow was the general manager of the Yankees from 1920 to 1945 (he added the title of club president in 1939). As the general manager, his job was to choose all the team's players and hire the field manager. He set salaries, planned games, and ran the ball club for its owner, Jacob Ruppert. Under Barrow's watch, the Yankees were a dominant force. Barrow was a quiet and thoughtful baseball man, who let Ruppert be the face of the team. Barrow also was one of the best judges of baseball talent ever. He could spot a future star in a young player, and he was expert at mixing veterans and **rookies** to create winning teams. Under him, the Yankees won fourteen American League **pennants** and ten World Series championships. He was inducted into the **National Baseball Hall of Fame** in 1953.

Ed Barrow was an excellent judge of baseball talent.

CHAPTER 4

Lou, the Yankee

Now playing first base, Lou Gehrig.

—*Yankee Stadium announcement*

In the spring of 1923, big, strapping Lou Gehrig arrived at Yankee Stadium to begin one of baseball's finest careers. As he stepped off the subway next to the enormous ballpark, he must have looked up. Amid a neighborhood of small, tightly packed houses and shops, the new building was tall, and it drew attention. The stadium towered over everything around it and was topped by a wide band of shining copper. Open just a few months when "Columbia Lou" showed up, it would become known as The House That Ruth Built. George Herman "Babe" Ruth was the Yankees'—and baseball's— leading man. His mighty home runs and outsized personality had made him a household name. Just two years earlier, he had hit 59 home runs to set a single-season record. He was the unchallenged king of the

Lou Gehrig joined the New York Yankees in 1923. In this photograph Gehrig models his new Yankee pinstripes.

Yankees. Young Lou was about to challenge that reign. Unlike the mature and professional players around him, however, Gehrig arrived with his baseball shoes (called spikes) and glove wrapped in newspaper, as if packed by his mother.

The Yankees wanted to take a closer look at the young man they had just signed to join their team. Manager Miller Huggins met Gehrig in the locker room and told him to take **batting practice (B.P.)**. Many stories about Gehrig over the years reported that he grabbed Ruth's bat, not having one of his own, for his first batting practice. Whether that is true or not, everyone does agree that Gehrig put on a show in B.P., launching several big homers into the right-field seats. Even veterans that were used to rookies trying to show off were impressed. "We knew he was a big-league ballplayer in the making. Nobody could miss him," said pitcher Waite Hoyt of Gehrig's first practice appearance.

Pitcher Waite Hoyt was one of the veteran Yankees who recognized Gehrig's potential.

Gehrig just hung around during that game and for several more. He was there mostly to practice, watch, listen, and learn. However, he did make his major-league debut on June 15, 1923, filling in at first base for an inning. A few days later, he struck out in his first big-league at bat. Although he made his first hit in a game in July, Gehrig was sent to the minor leagues. With the Yankees, he would not be able to play very often. In the minors, he could have more playing time and improve his skills. As good as he was in college, Gehrig was not quite ready to join the major leagues full time. Still, during his brief summer visit, he had impressed his teammates with his powerful bat and quiet manner. He was sent back to Hartford, where two years earlier his playing had caused trouble with Columbia (the Hartford team had become part of the Yankees organization). Now he could play and be paid openly and honestly. He was a professional ballplayer.

A Few Firsts

Life in Hartford was hard for young Lou. Living on his own was a huge adjustment after twenty years of living with his parents and having his mother do everything for him. He had had a brief time away in his short first time in Hartford, but this was the first long-term stay away from the comforts of home. Even when he was in college, his mother had taken care of him. Now, suddenly, he had to cook and clean for himself; he had to make sure he went where he was supposed to be; and he had to fit in with a group of strangers. All those were things that Gehrig was not too good at. "He was a guy who needed friends but didn't know how to go about getting them," said Harry Hesse, a Hartford teammate. "He'd get low and hunched over and miserable, and it was pretty tough to pull him out of it."

Gehrig's struggles extended to the ball field where he did not play his best for several weeks. However, he gradually drew himself out of his slump. He found friends on the team who shared his interests in focusing on baseball and not going out every night, which was the usual ballplayers' habit. By the end of the season in late September, he was hitting above .300; he even pitched and won a game.

Manager Miller Huggins had great talent on his team, and he knew how to make them winners.

Gehrig was called back to the Yankees after Hartford's season ended in early September. He played a few games as the Yankees wrapped up another pennant-winning season and hit his first major-league home run in late September. With a World Series against the Giants ahead, manager Miller Huggins wanted Gehrig to stay with the team. First baseman Wally Pipp had hurt his ankle, and Huggins wanted young Gehrig on the bench just in case Pipp couldn't play. However, baseball rules at the time said that a player must have been with the team by the end of August to qualify to play in the Series. Huggins asked for the rule to be waived, but the Giants' manager, John McGraw, objected, so Lou was not allowed to join the Yankees for the Series.

A Baseball Education

Gehrig reported for spring training with the Yankees in 1924 in New Orleans. He had worked as an office clerk at the Edison Company in the off-season, so he had a little money in his pocket—but not enough. Gehrig had no idea what life was like in this annual preseason camp. He thought he'd be able to work part-time while he took part in training. For a while, Gehrig actually looked for an evening job to make money, because players were not paid their full salary until the regular season started. However, there was no time, and in fact, no players worked at anything other than baseball during training camp. Older players knew to save money for use during training. Fortunately for Gehrig, a newspaper writer named Fred Lieb took pity on the confused youngster. Through Lieb's connections with the Yankees' management, he arranged for the team to give Gehrig an advance on the player's pay. Huggins also arranged for him to stay in a hotel room with two veteran players who could help Gehrig learn how to deal with camp life. Still, it was not easy for a young player in those days. Veterans took great delight in teasing and bothering the rookies. Gehrig reported that he once found one of his favorite bats sawed into four pieces. "They were sullen toward the rookies," he said. "They made it hard for us. If you weren't one of the [veterans], you didn't get a break on or off the field."

After playing a few games with the Yankees to start the 1924 season, Gehrig was sent again to the minors in Hartford, where he could play every day. Gehrig had a fantastic year, hitting 37 homers and 40 doubles while batting .369. He did, however, make more than 20 **errors** while playing first base, more than a veteran first baseman would.

He had another brief turn with the Yankees at the end of September. During those few games, he demonstrated that there was another part of baseball that he had to learn: how to keep his cool. Ballplayers are famous for their heckling, that is, making fun of other players during games. Hall-of-Fame outfielder Ty Cobb of the Detroit Tigers was especially good at this. In a late-season game against the Yankees, he got under Gehrig's skin with a variety of comments. Using bad language, he would make fun of Gehrig for being young, tease him about his mother,

Spring Training

When Gehrig and the rest of the Yankees went south for spring training, they were, in most cases, using that time to get into shape. They had been busy working at other jobs in the off-season, whether in an office, in construction, or on a farm. Few had time or interest in working out or going to a gym. So, the weeks spent in training were time for running sprints, taking batting practice, exercising, and losing their winter fat. Today, baseball players are expected to keep their bodies in top shape all year. Spring training is seen today more as a tryout for younger players, a checkup on players returning from injury, and a warm-up for players to regain their timing. Training methods, too, are different. In Gehrig's day, coaches frowned upon weightlifting. They were afraid that players would become too muscular and not stay flexible. Modern training methods, of course, allow players to do both.

Gehrig is on the far right of this group of Yankees as they wave from their train car before heading south for spring training.

and suggest that Gehrig was cowardly. Gehrig charged out of the dugout to fight Cobb; instead, Gehrig was kicked out of the game by the umpires. Another lesson learned: Don't listen to the hecklers.

Lou's on First

By the start of the 1925 season, Gehrig had progressed as far as he could in the minor leagues. He was more than ready to take his place as a regular on the Yankees. He stayed with the team as it headed north after spring training. However, the Yankees already had a solid first baseman, Wally Pipp, so Gehrig was a **pinch hitter** and Pipp's defensive substitute for several months. That would not last the summer, though.

Many books claim that on June 2, 1925, Pipp had a headache, was taken out of the lineup, and was replaced by Gehrig—who began that day the amazing streak of consecutive games played that would make him famous—and that Pipp never played again. Recent myth busters have shown that the "headache" was more legend than fact. Pipp was actually one of several Yankees' regulars taken out of the lineup that day in an effort

The unlucky Wally Pipp: His "headache" opened the door for Gehrig to begin "the Streak."

Wally Pipp (1893–1965)

First baseman Wally Pipp gained baseball fame not for the games he played, but for the one game he missed. After Gehrig replaced him in the lineup on June 2, 1925, he never started again for the Yankees. To this day, if a player is taken out and replaced by a young star, people say that he has been "Pipped." Wally Pipp was a pretty good player, actually. He led the American League in home runs twice and had 114 runs batted in (RBI) in 1924. He helped the Yankees win American League championships in 1921, 1922, and 1923. After the 1925 season, when Gehrig took over, Pipp moved to the Cincinnati Reds, where he played three more seasons before retiring.

by manager Miller Huggins to shake up the offense. No article of the time mentions that Pipp had a headache or any other ailment. Additionally, Gehrig's streak of games played actually started the day before, when he had appeared as a pinch hitter. Baseball history is full of legends, and Pipp's headache is one of them. However, a month after Gehrig took his place, Pipp was beaned (hit in the head by a pitch) during batting practice. He missed a month of playing and was never really the same. In the meantime, Gehrig established himself as the Yankees' new first baseman.

As the summer went along, Gehrig's parents became more and more accepting that their son would not become an engineer. They even began making regular trips to Yankee Stadium to see their son play. The regular paychecks he was receiving were more than most twenty-two-year-olds were making. Gehrig himself was proud. He knew that he was succeeding at his chosen profession. It was not the job of his parents' dreams, but he was a success, he was working hard, and he was paid a good salary. It is believed that Gehrig was so pleased with reaching his goal that he kept a newspaper clipping about his initial start at first base in his wallet for the rest of his life.

Lou and the Babe

Gehrig was adding another important relationship to his life—his relationship with Babe Ruth. When Gehrig joined the team in 1925, Ruth was clearly "the man" on the Yankees. He had a huge, oversized personality. While he was loud and crude, Gehrig was quiet and polite. While Ruth loved publicity, Gehrig

Ruth and Gehrig, shown here before a game at Yankee Stadium, became the greatest one-two punch in baseball history.

avoided it. While Ruth loved to break rules, Gehrig wanted to follow them. However, as the two best players on one of the biggest teams in sports, it was natural that they would be linked. Gehrig became more and more successful, while Ruth remained outstanding, so the press made them a "team of two." Gehrig, meanwhile, always understood where he was in the relationship.

"It's a pretty big shadow," he said. "It gives me lots of room to spread out. Let's face it, I'm not a big headline guy. I always knew that as long as I was following the Babe to the plate, I could have gone up there and stood on my head. No one would have noticed. When the Babe was through swinging, whether he hit or fanned [struck out], nobody paid any attention to the next hitter. They were all talking about Babe."

To the Series

In St. Petersburg, Florida, for spring training in 1926, the Yankees were surprised by an additional member of their party: Christina Gehrig. Most players enjoyed the freedom of spring training. After long days of training and working out, they stayed out late, drank too much, and enjoyed the nightlife. Lou Gehrig, on the other hand, spent time with his mom. In addition, when he was with her, he only spoke German, which his teammates did not understand. Meanwhile, Christina made friends with Mary Lieb, the wife of sportswriter Fred Lieb, who followed the team wherever they went. The Liebs' kindness to Christina made them and Lou Gehrig close friends.

Gehrig was a key part of the Yankees' 1926 team, sharing the third and fourth spots in the batting order with Ruth and playing first base in every game. Though he improved all his stats (he would end the season with 112 RBI, the first of thirteen straight seasons in which he had more than 100 RBI), he remained a

Sportswriter Fred Lieb (center) became a close friend of Gehrig and his family.

bit of a kid. Teammates teased him when he brought cookies or pickled eels from his mom to the clubhouse. He sometimes cried, sitting on the bench, if he made an out in a key situation. Still, his no-nonsense attitude about the game—don't talk, play hard, play to win—was appreciated by management. "Lou has become an influence to the entire team," Huggins said. "You get a player with that kind of spirit and it spreads . . . to other players."

Though only twenty-three years old and in his second full season, Gehrig was a team leader. The club had rookies at second base and shortstop—Tony Lazzeri and Mark Koenig. It also still had the mighty Ruth, who batted .372 with 47 homers and

The Yankees 1926 infield: Gehrig, Tony Lazzeri, Mark Koenig, and Joe Dugan.

150 RBI. Huggins guided his power duo of Ruth and Gehrig and his raw youngsters to the 1926 A.L. pennant. Lou Gehrig would play in his first World Series!

New York faced the St. Louis Cardinals, champions of the National League, who were led by future Hall-of-Famer Rogers Hornsby at second base and by pitcher Grover Cleveland "Pete" Alexander. Ruth hit four homers in the seven-game series, while Lou batted .348. After each team won three games, it came down to a seventh and deciding contest. In the seventh inning of this final game, Alexander was called from the **bullpen** as a relief pitcher, although he had pitched a complete game the day before. (Most pitchers are not physically able to pitch two days

The Cardinals' second baseman, Rogers Hornsby (left), wishes his former manager, Miller Huggins, good luck before the Cardinals and Yankees face off in the 1926 World Series.

in a row, especially if they pitched several innings on the first day.) In one of the World Series' most memorable moments, with the Yankees trailing 3–2, Alexander struck out hot-hitting Lazzeri with the bases loaded to preserve the Cardinals' lead. In the ninth inning, the Yankees had another chance to tie the score, but amazingly, it was Ruth who made a big mistake. With powerful outfielder Bob Meusel at bat and two outs, Ruth tried to steal second base (that is, run as the pitcher threw the ball instead of waiting until Ruth's teammate hit the ball). Instead of making it safely, he was tagged out to end the game and give the Cardinals the championship.

CHAPTER 5

1927

The most astonishing thing that has ever happened in organized baseball is the home run race between George Herman Ruth and Henry Louis Gehrig.

—Paul Gallico

When baseball historians debate what is the greatest team of all time, the 1927 New York Yankees are nearly always at or near the top. They simply dominated the American League that year, putting up numbers that still astound fans.

The Yankees' 158 homers were the most ever by a team to that point, and Ruth's 60 home runs topped every other *team* in the entire American League. They won the pennant by nineteen games. Six players would eventually join the Hall of Fame: Gehrig, Ruth, Lazzeri, Hoyt, outfielder Earle Combs, and pitcher Herb Pennock. Manager Huggins made it in, too.

The outfield was incredible. Meusel was one of the game's best fielders and a powerful hitter. Combs hit .356 and got on base regularly while batting first in the order (also known as the leadoff position). Ruth owned right field. The infield included Gehrig at first base, Lazzeri at second, Koenig at shortstop, and "Jumpin'" Joe Dugan at third. The catchers, oddly, were a **motley crew** of players who didn't contribute nearly as much.

Every pitcher's nightmare: Murderers' Row—Gehrig, Bob Meusel, Tony Lazzeri, and Babe Ruth.

In the batting order, the quartet of Meusel, Gehrig, Ruth, and Lazzeri had earned a memorable nickname for its ability to pound the ball: Murderers' Row.

On the pitching staff, Hoyt won twenty-two games, Pennock and Wilcy Moore nineteen each, and Urban Shocker another eighteen. The team didn't need a deep bullpen, because it was often comfortably ahead late in most games. However, when the Yankees did have to come from behind, they often called on rallies known as Five O'clock Lightning, after the time of day they usually happened. If the Yankees were trailing, they would often come up with enough runs to win late in the game. (Most games started at three o'clock, so the Yankees' late-inning heroics often came around five o'clock, or roughly two hours into the game.)

Gehrig finishes a swing during batting practice. His left-handed power stroke was perfect for Yankee Stadium.

For his part, Gehrig smacked 47 homers and set a new major-league record (later broken by himself and others) with 175 RBI. He batted .373 with 18 triples and led the league with 52 doubles. Gehrig was voted the league's most valuable player (MVP) for that year. (Ruth, as a prior MVP winner, was not eligible to win again, according to the rules of that time.)

The Home Run Race

As the season went along, it became more and more clear that no one could challenge the Yankees for the league pennant. However, another race was beginning that would hold the attention of baseball fans throughout the summer. In 1921, Babe Ruth clubbed an amazing 59 homers. No player ever really challenged that mark . . . until 1927. That summer, as Ruth continued to send baseball after baseball into the seats, he had company. Gehrig nearly matched Ruth and a home-run "race" was on.

On July 1, the duo was tied with 25 homers each. By late August, they were still neck and neck. Fans were thrilled by what was called the Great Home Run Derby by the press. At this time in baseball, with the exception of Ruth and now Gehrig, very few players were big home-run hitters. For instance, in this season in which Ruth and Gehrig hit 107 homers between them, Lazzeri

was third in the league . . . with 18.
Only two National League players
reached 30 home runs during that
season: Ken Williams and Hack
Wilson. Only two others even
reached 20. So for Ruth and Gehrig
to do what they were doing, on the
same team, back-to-back in some
cases, was simply stunning.

"The most astonishing thing
that has ever happened in organized
baseball is the home run race
between George Herman Ruth
and Henry Louis Gehrig," Paul
Gallico wrote.

Babe Ruth's popularity was
enormous; he is shown here
on the cover of a *Who's Who
in Baseball.*

Still, Gehrig, in his modest way,
downplayed the feat. "I have as much respect for the home
run as anybody," he said, "but I like straightaway hitting. I
believe it's the proper way to hit. A lot of home runs are lucky.
There's nothing lucky about a solid smash, straight out over
the [infield]."

However, fans go wild for the home run, then and now.
The battle for the home-run crown—and the chase after Ruth's
1921 record of 59—continued. As late as September 6, the two
players were tied at 44 each. From then on, Ruth hit 16 more,
while Gehrig managed only 3. Most experts point to Gehrig's
mom as the reason. Late in the season, and even through the
World Series, she became very ill (she later recovered fully from
what was probably a stomach ailment) and was in the hospital.
Gehrig was extremely worried about her, so he had trouble
concentrating on his game. In the final month of the season,

Gehrig's batting average dipped 50 points, and he made 4 errors. Meanwhile, the Yankees did everything they could to assure him Christina was well cared for. They couldn't afford to have their slugger sitting in her hospital room as they battled for the championship.

On the second-to-last day of the season, Ruth hit home run number 60. It was a record that would stand for thirty-four years. Gehrig hit 47 homers that season—29 more than anyone else in the league, except Ruth.

. . . the Yankees did everything they could to assure him Christina was well cared for. They couldn't afford to have their slugger sitting in her hospital room as they battled for the championship.

However, Ruth's record left Gehrig in his shadow, as always.

The competition between the two teammates was on the field. Off the field, they were friendly but not close. Because they were linked by their home runs, most assumed a closeness that wasn't there. Gehrig and Ruth were very different sorts of people with very different points of view on life. For instance, Gehrig backed Huggins 100 percent, while Ruth just didn't like being told what to do. As such, their greatest moments as a pair all came on the field, not off it.

Babe Ruth did not play saxophone, but he attempted to for this photograph as Gehrig tried not to listen.

Ruth Versus the Rest

Babe Ruth's 1927 record of 60 homers in one season lasted until Roger Maris of the Yankees hit 61 in 1961. In 1998, Mark McGwire of the St. Louis Cardinals and Sammy Sosa of the Chicago Cubs repeated the home-run race of Ruth and Gehrig. In the end, both topped Maris's mark, with McGwire setting the new record at 70 and Sosa reaching 66. In 2002, Barry Bonds raised the bar even further, reaching 73. All those records after Maris have been called into question due to suspicion that the players used drugs called steroids to make themselves stronger. (Major League Baseball had banned the use of steroids used to enhance players' abilities.) However, drug use has not been proven, and Bonds's record stand.

Barry Bonds watches his record-breaking 71st home run fly out of the ballpark.

For his part, Gehrig knew what he could learn from his older, worldly teammate. During a tour they would take after the 1927 season, he said. "Babe sure knows how to live. [This trip] was the most wonderful education I've ever been given. I don't mean in books. I mean in getting the most out of life, in learning to meet people and having a good time and really seeing all there is to see."

Ruth certainly respected Gehrig's talents. After hitting 60 homers in 1927, Ruth was asked if anyone would ever break the mark. "I don't know, and I don't care," he said. "But if I don't beat it myself, I know who will. Wait until that guy over there [pointing to Gehrig] wades into them; they may forget a guy named Ruth ever lived."

The Yankees Sweep

After waltzing through the American League, the Yankees took on the National League's Pittsburgh Pirates in the World Series. They kicked things off with a batting practice display that is still legendary. In those days, there was no interleague play other than in the World Series and no television highlights of games, so few Pirates had actually seen Ruth, Gehrig, and the rest of Murderer's Row in person, at least not that season. They stood open-mouthed as the Yankees pounded baseball after baseball into the seats during pregame practice. Ring Lardner, one of America's finest writers, wrote at the time, "I don't mean to imply that the Pirates are scared, but if they ain't nervous, they ain't human."

The Pirates boasted a fine set of outfielders, brothers Paul and Lloyd Waner, who would both go into the Hall of Fame. They had won the National League over a tough Cardinals team led by another Hall of Famer, Frankie Frisch. However,

A 1927 World Series program (above) features the managers of the Yankees and Pirates. At right is a ticket for Game 3 of that Series.

they were still no match for Gehrig and the rest of the team. The Yankees won Game 1 of the Series 5–4 as Gehrig had two RBI. They won the second game 6–2. In New York for Game 3, Gehrig had two more RBI on a triple in an easy 8–1 win. Oddly, in Game 4, on October 8, 1927, the Yankees' winning run did not come on a blast by Gehrig, a homer by Ruth, or even a slugging double by Meusel or Lazzeri. With the scored tied 3–3 in the ninth inning and the bases loaded, Earle Combs scored on a **wild pitch**. The Yankees had completed their amazing season with the first A.L. sweep (winning four games in a row) of a World Series. Even better news for Lou and his teammates was that each player would receive another $5,592 for winning the title. As Gehrig's salary for that season was $8,000, that was quite a bonus. It would not be the last time, though, that he earned such a big postseason check.

CHAPTER 6

Lou's Big Years

*Gehrig is certainly one of the Yanks' prize
locomotives—an . . . Iron Horse.*
—Will Wedge

Baseball players in Gehrig's time usually didn't depend on the salaries paid by the teams. Most also had off-season jobs. Gehrig was a clerk and a salesman, for instance. However, once Gehrig became a superstar player in 1927, another off-season job opened up: playing baseball. However, the baseball he played in the off-season didn't count in the official standings. These games were played more to entertain fans than to keep count of wins and losses. The exhibition games were known as "barnstorming," and were actually against the rules for members of World Series teams until the mid-1920s. Team owners thought that players should only play for their teams, not for these exhibition teams. After Ruth and others broke the rule and traveled around the country playing games in these barnstorming tours anyway, baseball adjusted and allowed the trips.

The way barnstorming worked was that a **promoter** would schedule games in cities near railroad lines. Then he would hire professional players to take part in the games. Local organizers would sell tickets to a game, in which the stars would be matched against a local team or would be mixed in with local players. The stars would be paid most of the ticket money, sign some autographs, and then hop onto the train to the next city.

Christy Walsh, Ruth's business manager, organized several such tours. The first big one was in 1927. Walsh created two "teams": the Bustin' Babes and the Larrupin' Lous. Gehrig's team name was a play on a cowboy term, as several of the games were to be played in the West. At this point, no town west of St. Louis, Missouri, had a major-league baseball team—and there was no television on which people could watch East Coast games. Most fans in the West only saw their heroes in photographs or sometimes in **newsreels** in movie theaters. When Ruth and Gehrig came into town, it was big news. It was also big business.

Christy Walsh (in suit) and Gehrig (in white) pose with the traveling "Bustin' Babes" ball team, headed by Ruth (to the right of Walsh).

On this tour, Gehrig and Ruth joined local teams while playing sixteen games in fourteen days and traveling eight thousand miles. Stops included Denver, Colorado, as well as San Francisco and other California cities. In Los Angeles, thirty thousand people turned out to see the two stars play ball. At one stop, fans were so excited to see the players that they swarmed the field, and the game could not be completed.

Gehrig's Money

On that 1927 tour, Ruth took home about $30,000 while Gehrig received $10,000, "all of which he intended to turn over to his mother."

However, still concerned about money, Gehrig sold life insurance during the rest of that off-season. Throughout his life, Gehrig worried about money. He saved much of it or gave it to his parents. He did not spend a lot on cars or parties or jewelry as many other highly paid athletes did. Even though he should have been comfortable, his personality was such that money was always a concern for him.

How he dealt with money also affected how he dealt with Ruth. In fact, the two disagreed often about money. Gehrig was famously stingy, rarely spending money. On the other hand, he was also very loyal to the Yankees and didn't want to ask for a raise. Ruth knew about all this and teased Gehrig often.

> *Even though he should have been comfortable, his personality was such that money was always a concern for him.*

"Hey Dutchman [another Gehrig nickname], didn't I get you $10,000 for that trip in 1927?" Gehrig nodded. "Wasn't that more money than you made all year from the Yankees?" Gehrig nodded again. Later, before the 1928 season, Ruth made Gehrig promise to hold out for $30,000, which Ruth hoped would lead to even more money for him. Without telling Ruth, Gehrig signed a contract that would pay him $25,000 for each of the next three years. Ruth was angry. "Why didn't you keep your promise?" he asked Gehrig. Gehrig, however, was satisfied with his raise.

One benefit of all his newfound wealth meant that Gehrig could move his parents out of their small apartment in Manhattan. He bought a four-bedroom house for them in New Rochelle, a city about thirty miles north of Manhattan. Yorkville was where the Gehrigs had started out, comfortably surrounded by their fellow German immigrants. Once they could afford to leave, they did so gladly. Their new home was a palace compared to the small apartment where Gehrig grew up.

Also taking up residence in the house: Lou Gehrig, baseball superstar. Despite being able to support himself, Gehrig continued to live at home with his parents. In fact, clubhouse attendant Pete Sheehy had the job of calling Gehrig's mom every game day to let her know if the game would be played or if rain would postpone it. (Gehrig wasn't the only one to rely on his mom. Among many others, shortstop Frank Crosetti went to Christina for homemade cold medicine.)

Though he was twenty-five years old in 1928, Lou Gehrig was in some ways still a kid. For example, to keep his star player from being injured, general manager Barrow once had to tell Gehrig to stop playing stickball, a street baseball game played with a rubber ball and a broomstick, with the kids in his neighborhood. In fact, during one of those evening games, a ball flew through a window, shattering it. An annoyed resident called the police. They arrived quickly, only to find one of New York's finest ballplayers helping to clean up the glass.

Stickball was played on the city streets with a rubber ball and a broomstick for a bat. Gehrig was sometimes seen taking a few swings on his way home from Yankee Stadium.

Gehrig remained uncomfortable talking to writers about his successes. He still hung out more with his parents than his teammates. He was afraid to ask for more money from the Yankees, though he had certainly earned it. He made sure to sign each contract they mailed to him as soon as he got it, never trying to ask for a raise as most very successful players did. (In 1927, when he was paid $8,000, Ruth earned $70,000—nearly ten times more.) Gehrig was respected for his great talent and his all-out play. However, teammates, fans, and writers found him to be shy, quiet, and hard to know.

Another Series Sweep

The Yankees continued their dominance of the American League in 1928. The Philadelphia Athletics did press them a bit, making the run for league champion close near the end of the season. However, a big set of games won in September by New York took Philadelphia out of the competition and sent the Yankees to the World Series once again. Gehrig continued to amaze fans throughout the 1928 season. He posted the second-highest batting average of his career, .374, while knocking in 142 runs. Ruth tied him for the RBI crown and hit 54 homers to Gehrig's 27.

In the World Series, baseball saw another example of Ruth being just great enough to knock an almost equally great Gehrig out of the top spot. In a four-game sweep of the Cardinals, Ruth hit .625; Gehrig, .545. Ruth had a record ten hits; Gehrig, a record nine RBI. Gehrig tied Ruth's previous record by hitting four homers in the Series. Ruth stole that thunder, too, by becoming the first player with three home runs in one Series game in the Series-clinching Game 4.

Together, however, they were titanic, batting a combined .593 with 7 homers and 13 RBI—all in just four games. It was an incredible show, another chapter in this two-of-a-kind baseball tale.

This ticket admitted a fan to one of the games in the 1928 World Series. The Yankees swept the Cardinals that year.

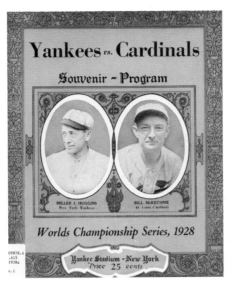

A great souvenir for a lucky fan: the 1928 World Series program. Pictured on it are the managers of the Yankees and Cardinals.

A Tragic Season

The following year, 1929, was a tough one all around for the Yankees. The team became one of the first clubs to wear numbers on its uniforms (Gehrig wore number 4) but otherwise did not lead the league that year. Meusel sank to .261 in his last season in Yankees' pinstripes. Pitchers Hoyt and Pennock plummeted, combining to win twenty-one fewer games than in 1928. Gehrig batted only .300, an uncharacteristically low average.

Baseball was touched by tragedy, as Ruth's wife was killed in a house fire in January of that season. When a storm caused fans to stampede out of Yankee Stadium in May, two of them were trampled by the crowd and killed.

Around the league, more and more teams were feeling the effects of an **economic** slump that was swirling in America. It

Why No. 4?

Lou Gehrig wore uniform number 4 because he batted fourth in the lineup. It was not until 1929 that the Yankees became the second team to wear numbers on their uniforms. (The Cleveland Indians, who opened their season just two days earlier, also added numbers that year.) The Yankees used the batting order to assign the numbers, so Ruth was number 3 and Gehrig, number 4. (Today, numbers are assigned randomly or by player choice.) In recognition of Ruth's and Gehrig's great careers, those two numbers were retired and will never be worn by a Yankees' player again. In fact, the Yankees have retired fifteen numbers—more than any other team. Based on his surefire Hall of Fame career, current Yankees captain Derek Jeter's No. 2 will likely join them someday. Many teams choose to retire numbers to honor their greatest heroes.

Gehrig's No. 4 jersey is on display at the Baseball Hall of Fame.

would reach its peak just after the season with the crash of the **stock market** in October 1929, sending millions into poverty and ruining many lives. The event was the beginning of a long, worldwide period of financial struggle called the Great Depression.

Amid all this, the Yankees faced their greatest tragedy, the loss of their leader. In September, after having been sick for five days, Miller Huggins died of a skin disease that had become infected. Huggins's death shocked the team, perhaps Gehrig most deeply. Huggins was only fifty-one and had been Gehrig's only manager in the majors, the man who had guided him into this new world of pro baseball.

Though he clashed often with Ruth, Huggins got along very well with Gehrig. While Ruth wanted to be the center of

In this 1929 photograph, Babe Ruth and Gehrig sit on either side of little Miller Huggins, the longtime Yankee manager.

The Great Depression

In the fall of 1929, the stock market suddenly lost enormous amounts of value, and millions of people lost most or all of the money they had invested. Because of this, thousands of businesses failed, hundreds of banks closed, and many people lost their jobs. In a very short time, much of America was in terrible economic trouble—the Great Depression.

It would last for several years as people scrambled to find work or even to feed and house their families. The economy gradually recovered, helped in large part by new programs put in place starting in 1933 by the newly elected president, Franklin Roosevelt. Still, the Depression left a large scar on America and its people.

Amid the panic of the 1929 stock market crash, people lined up at banks trying to get their money out.

attention and always have his way, Gehrig was a team player and loyal to the bosses. Gehrig treated Huggins almost as a father figure, worrying about disappointing him even as he slugged homer after homer and never missed a game. When Huggins died so suddenly, Gehrig was very upset.

After Huggins's funeral, Gehrig told reporters, "I guess I'll miss him more than anyone else. Next to my mother and father, he was the best friend a boy could have. He taught me everything I know. Because of him, I had everything a man could ask for in a material way. I can't believe he'll never join us again."

Two Super Seasons

Fans watched Gehrig put up stunning stat after stunning stat. Few believed that he (and Ruth) could do any more. In 1930 and 1931, they did just that, Gehrig especially. In an era that included some of the finest hitters of all time in their prime—Rogers Hornsby, Al Simmons, Jimmie Foxx, and Hank Greenberg, among others—Gehrig outshone almost all of them. In 1930, he posted a career-high .379 average with 41 homers and 174 RBI. Ruth was no slouch himself, with a .359 average, 49 homers, and 153 RBI.

In 1930, Gehrig also added another reason for fans to cheer him on. That season, Joe Sewell of the Cleveland Indians ended his streak after playing in 1,103 straight games, without missing a single one. Gehrig suddenly had baseball's longest active streak at 744 games. Thanks to the awareness by the press of this feat, Gehrig earned (in 1931) his most famous nickname, courtesy of Will Wedge of the New York Sun: "Gehrig is certainly one of the Yanks' prize locomotives—an . . . Iron Horse." Immediately after the 1930 season, though, Gehrig was in a hospital. He had a broken pinky and bone chips in his elbow, and he needed

Miller Huggins (1879–1929)

A scrappy infielder who had played for the Cincinnati Reds and one of only a handful of ballplayers to graduate law school, Miller Huggins was the manager of the Yankees during their greatest years. He took over the team in 1918 and led them until his death in 1929. During those years, New York won six American League pennants and three World Series (1923, 1927, and 1928). Huggins had the impressive ability of finding the most in his star players. Managing a team with many great players can be a challenge. And keeping them all happy can be nearly impossible. The tough-minded Huggins molded his stars into a series of awesome teams. Huggins was elected to the Hall of Fame in 1964.

Huggins's sudden death was devastating to Gehrig.

Weeks after the 1930 season ended, Gehrig was in the hospital for several small surgeries to repair nagging injuries.

surgery. It's hard to believe he had played the previous three weeks with such injuries. It was truly an Iron Horse performance.

Fully healthy for the 1931 season, Gehrig had an even better year. He whacked 46 homers to tie Ruth for the most in the league and batted .341. More importantly, his 184 RBI were the A.L. record, and he led the league with 211 hits. On top of all of that, he scored a career-high 163 runs. In addition, he did all this in just 155 games, a full schedule in those days (it's 162 today). However, the team still couldn't overcome the mighty Athletics and finished a surprising thirteen games behind first-place Philadelphia in the A.L. pennant race.

An interesting off season note is that Gehrig, along with sports writer Fred Lieb and his wife Mary, Babe Ruth, and future Hall of Famers, such as Lefty Grove and Mickey Cochrane, traveled to Japan for several weeks to play exhibition baseball. It was not the last trip there for Gehrig—the next one would have a much bigger impact on his life.

Two Very Different Men

As evidence of the Great Depression, Gehrig, Ruth, and others were actually paid less the season after their outburst of offensive excellence. The Great Depression had hit baseball, too. Fewer fans were going to games, and owners had less money to pay players. Gehrig took a $2,000 salary cut to $23,000.

Meanwhile, the differences between Gehrig and Ruth continued. Gehrig loved playing for Huggins, while Ruth often gave the manager trouble. Now, in 1931, Joe McCarthy had taken over as manager. Still, Gehrig followed the team rules and always backed the manager. McCarthy recognized that and praised Gehrig. He knew the value of Gehrig not only as a talented player, but also

Gehrig loved playing for Huggins, while Ruth often gave the manager trouble.

as a coachable teammate. "What a wonderful fellow that Gehrig was!" he said later. "Always hustled. Never gave a moment's trouble. Just went out every day and played his game and hit the ball."

Ruth was a different story. McCarthy was a real stickler for rules, demanding that players always wear coats and ties and act properly in public. Ruth, of course, didn't want to do either— acting up was a big part of his fun. Gehrig, for his part, loved the order and discipline. On a train trip, Ruth made fun of McCarthy's leadership style. In a rare burst of anger, Gehrig hotly defended the manager. Thanks to made-up newspaper stories and agents who spread positive, if untrue, tales, the public saw Ruth and Gehrig as close friends. In reality, they were probably growing apart from each other.

Gehrig and manager Joe McCarthy share a laugh in the Yankee dugout.

Back to the Top

The Philadelphia Athletics had become the cream of the American League since 1929, boasting their own trio of Hall-of-Fame hitters: Al Simmons, Mickey Cochrane, and Jimmie Foxx. They also had the amazing Lefty Grove as their ace, or No. 1, starting pitcher. By 1932, however, a few new players had joined Ruth and Gehrig to push the Yankees back on top. Bill Dickey had taken over as catcher and proved to be a solid hitter as well. The soft-spoken Dickey also quickly became Gehrig's best friend on the team. Speedy Ben Chapman joined Ruth in the outfield, and often set up RBI chances for the sluggers who followed him. Red Ruffing and Lefty Gomez stepped in as the aces of the Yankees' pitching staff. Though

Catcher Bill Dickey became one of Gehrig's closest friends on the Yankees.

the Athletics' Foxx nearly matched Ruth's record by hitting 58 homers, the Yankees romped to the pennant by thirteen games.

Gehrig again had an awesome year, batting .349 with 34 home runs and 151 RBI. Ruth, though he was thirty-seven and nearing the end of his legendary career, still knocked in 137 runs and batted .341.

A major highlight of the season for Gehrig came on June 3 in a game against the Yankees' rivals, the Athletics. Gehrig hit home runs in the first, fourth, and fifth innings, tying Ruth and many others for the most ever in one game since 1900. In the seventh inning, he crushed another. Gehrig was the first player

Gehrig had a short, compact swing that was almost technically perfect. This photo shows him finishing a swing with near-perfect form.

in the modern era (post-1900) to hit four homers in a game. Only twelve players since have matched the feat—and Babe Ruth was not one of them. Gehrig actually had a chance for a fifth home run on an inside-the-park possibility, but the Athletics' centerfielder Al Simmons tracked down and caught Gehrig's long drive in deepest center field.

The 1932 World Series was Babe Ruth's last hurrah in pinstripes. The Yankees faced the Chicago Cubs and easily won the first two games.

Members of the 1932 Yankees team each received one of these World Series championship rings.

In Game 3, Ruth whacked a homer after supposedly calling his shot. It's one of the most famous moments in World Series history. Fittingly, Gehrig stepped to the plate right after Ruth—and also hit a homer. Few remember that blast in the shadow of Ruth's magic moment. The Yankees went on to win the World Series in four games.

The Called Shot

The score was tied at 4–4 between the New York Yankees and the Chicago Cubs in the fifth inning of Game 3 of the 1932 World Series, when Babe Ruth stepped to the plate in Chicago's Wrigley Field. He'd already had a three-run homer in the game, and the Cubs were heckling him fiercely. The Wrigley fans added their voices to the din. Ruth took strike one and then held up one finger. He looked at strike two as it passed him. At this point, the story of what happened next mixes with legend. Before the next pitch, Ruth made some sort of gesture. Some say he was pointing to center field, others say to Charley Root, the pitcher. Others say he was simply holding up two fingers, to indicate that Root had only thrown two strikes. Still others say he was pointing to the Cubs' bench, telling them to be quiet. Whatever he did then, what he did next is not disputed. He crushed Root's next pitch into the center-field seats. He laughed and waved his hat and pointed at the Cubs' bench as he rounded the bases. Fans marveled and wondered if Ruth had "called his shot." It seemed to many that Ruth had pointed to the bleachers as if to say, "I'm hitting the next one right there" . . . and then did just that. To this day, fans, writers, and historians continue the debate. For his part, Ruth always said some version of, "It makes a great story, doesn't it?"

CHAPTER 7

Eleanor and Lou

Lou picked up the phone, called the mayor of New Rochelle, and told him to bring the marriage license—and make it fast!

—Eleanor Twitchell Gehrig

Lou Gehrig always had one woman in his life: Christina Gehrig. However, unlike most young men, and most young ballplayers, that was pretty much it. As he was with making friends, he was also shy and uncomfortable meeting women, even if they were just asking for an autograph. Along with that, Christina was a powerful personality who made it hard for Lou to bring women home to meet her. Several stories say that Lou met a couple of different women, but broke up with them after Christina disapproved. Always being compared to Ruth, Gehrig was nowhere near the ladies' man that Ruth was; this was yet another difference in their personalities.

In 1932 that changed. Through mutual friends, Gehrig met a woman from Chicago named Eleanor Twitchell. (He had actually been introduced to her briefly in 1928 before a game against the White Sox.) Lou Gehrig had met his match.

Meet Eleanor

When Eleanor Twitchell was a young woman growing up in Chicago in the 1920s, most of her time was spent

A portrait of the happy couple: Gehrig and Eleanor relax on the porch of their home.

trying to have fun. Her father was a successful business owner, so she could afford to enjoy herself. She loved to ride horses, go to dances, and attend parties. She learned to play poker and even smoked, which was rare among women in those days. She wore fashionable clothes and had a short haircut like several movie stars of the day. Eleanor was what was known then as a "flapper."

However, by the time Eleanor met Lou for the second time in 1932, her life had changed. She had left behind some of her wild ways. Her father's business, like that of so many people, had lost money in the Depression. Eleanor held a series of jobs working in offices. In addition, she was twenty-eight years old. For women of that era, it was past time for her to think about marriage. At that time, women were expected to marry fairly young, and if they waited too long, parents worried that their daughters would never marry. Eleanor had had her fun. It was time, she felt, to settle down. Lou Gehrig came along at just the right time.

Lou's New Teammate

After meeting Eleanor again at a party held at the apartment of a baseball-loving businessman in Chicago, Lou fell for her. Though he left Chicago soon after, he sent her a crystal necklace

Flappers

Following the horrors of World War I, America entered an era that is popularly called the Roaring '20s. More and more young people looked for fun instead of entering into what they deemed to be boring lives of business. They drank, smoked, and partied much more often. Women, in particular, took part as never before. They wore fringe-covered, straight-cut dresses. Unlike women of earlier years, they often kept their hair cut short. They danced all the new dances and made decisions for themselves (women just received the right to vote in 1920, too). Often these young women were called flappers. The name may have come from a comparison of the young women to young birds leaving their nests, flapping their wings as they went. However, not every word expert agrees with that source.

Flappers typically wore skirts of this length, long strings of beads or pearls, and had short haircuts.

when he arrived home. They hadn't even had an official date yet, so Eleanor was quite impressed. They wrote letters and notes back and forth for several months.

Lou and Eleanor saw each other again in May 1933, when the Yankees were in town to play the White Sox. The day after they had dinner with friends, he came to her office to take her out. A looming rainstorm meant that the baseball games would be postponed, and Lou would have plenty of time to spend with Eleanor. They sealed the deal with a kiss and started planning for the future.

"We went to the Drake Hotel [in Chicago] for breakfast," wrote Eleanor. "I don't remember who proposed to whom. We just plotted and planned. Everything, including the fact that his 'Mom would be hard to handle,' and so we even created a strategy for that problem."

Indeed, at some point, Lou let Christina know about Eleanor and even brought Mrs. Gehrig to Chicago to meet the young woman who had stolen his heart. Eleanor remembers Christina as being "built like a lady wrestler." Christina was unmoved by Eleanor, however. She didn't like her outgoing ways and her casual attitude. For example, she was shocked when asked to call Eleanor's mother by her first name, Nell. That was just not how people were supposed to act, thought Christina.

A Wild Wedding

In fact, when the wedding plans were announced for near the end of the 1933 baseball season, Christina declared flatly, "I'm not going to be there!" Fred Lieb was assigned the job of bringing Christina to the wedding. As it turned out, he didn't have to. When Eleanor again expressed her concern about Christina causing a scene at the wedding, Lou changed

Always supportive of Lou, Eleanor was a regular at Yankees games.

the play. He decided not to wait for the big wedding at the church.

On, September 29, 1933, Eleanor was home, amid the chaos of remodeling their soon-to-be apartment in a building not far from Lou's parents in New Rochelle. Carpenters, painters, plumbers, and other workers filled the house. Lou busted in to say that it was now or never.

Here's how Eleanor described the scene. "Lou picked up the phone, called the mayor of New Rochelle, and told him to bring the marriage license—and make it fast! The mayor did just that, accompanied by motorcycle cops." They were married in the living room as the construction stopped for a moment. Caps were removed, hammers put down, electric saws turned off. Mayor Otto did his job, champagne was poured, and that was that: Lou was a married man.

One more problem remained: Gehrig had a ball game in just about an hour. Mayor Otto came through again, dispatching his police officers to escort the Gehrigs to Yankee Stadium, sirens blaring all the way. It was a classic scene recreated in *The Pride of the Yankees*, the 1942 movie about Gehrig's life. For once, Hollywood didn't have to exaggerate very much.

> *Mayor Otto did his job, champagne was poured, and that was that: Lou was a married man.*

Eleanor's Effect

Before Eleanor, a big night out for Lou was a solo trip to the movies. With Eleanor in his life, a new world opened for him. She took him to Broadway shows and to the opera. They attended the ballet, at which Lou was very impressed with the athletic talents of the dancers. Eleanor exposed Lou to many great books; he was always a reader, but she introduced him to new and different writers.

She also recognized that Lou was selling himself short in the business world. After buying him new and fancier suits and shoes, she worked with agent Christy Walsh to encourage Lou to use his fame more often. In 1934, Lou was the first baseball player to appear on a Wheaties® cereal box. Other companies also paid him to promote their products. She even helped create the words for a song written about Lou.

In 1935, Eleanor and a songwriter friend wrote "I Can't Get to First Base With You." The song was supposed to take

Thanks to Eleanor, Gehrig became more interested in meeting his public. Here he is, signing copies of the sheet music for the song co-written by Eleanor.

advantage of Lou's popularity. Many other baseball-themed songs and movies were out at the time, and Eleanor wanted to join the fun. However, the song was not very good, and no well-known singers ever recorded it. The song didn't even use Lou's name as part of the lyrics.

Lou's mother was still central in his life. He saw her often, at her home and at the ballpark, where she attended games as much as she could. Eleanor was his wife and his partner, but Mrs. Gehrig still had her son's attention. For example, after Lou and Eleanor found they could not have children, they talked about adopting one. Christina objected so strongly, however, that they never followed through.

Gehrig's mother remained a strong presence in his life even after he got married. Christina (in glasses) was often seen at Yankee Stadium.

The Streak Appears

Meanwhile, on the field, Gehrig kept slugging (.334 average, 32 homers, and 139 RBI in 1933) and playing. On August 17, 1933, about a month before he married Eleanor, he became the all-time major-league leader for consecutive games played. By appearing in his 1,308th straight game, he topped the record of Everett Scott, a shortstop who had begun his career with the Boston Red Sox and was briefly Gehrig's teammate in New York.

It might surprise today's fans, who know every tiny bit of fact and trivia about their favorite players, that Gehrig's new status as the most durable player was somewhat of a surprise at the time. It had only been earlier in 1933 that Gehrig found out how close he was to the all-time record—when a sportswriter told him that he was closing in on it. Dan Daniel, a well-known

Gehrig was presented with a commemorative trophy for topping Everett Scott's consecutive-games-played record of 1,307.

writer for the *New York World Telegram*, had been counting some numbers. He told Gehrig and then the baseball world, that there was a new "iron man" in the game. On the day he topped Scott's mark, Gehrig received a trophy from the league in recognition of the feat, and congratulations poured in.

"I guess I must have been lucky," Gehrig said in an interview. "I suppose I can thank my sturdy German **ancestry** for this [ability]. Both my mother and father weighed over 200 pounds. We are a very big-boned family."

From that point on, "the Streak" began to define Gehrig. People kept track of how many games he had played in a row. When he became ill, fans worried that the Streak would end. Gehrig, however, kept playing and playing and playing.

CHAPTER 8

Championship Seasons

Lou was the perfect team man.

—Tommy Henrich

Marriage must have agreed with Gehrig. He was happier than he had ever been. Life with Eleanor was going swimmingly, and, beginning in 1935, the Yankees were truly "his" team as Ruth's stardom faded in New York. (Ruth would move on to the Boston Braves after the 1934 season.) In 1934, Gehrig won the Triple Crown, an honor given for leading the American League in homers (49), RBI (165), and batting average (.363). The Streak continued, too, as he overcame an ongoing assortment of bumps and bruises to play with his team day after day. One event, though, nearly brought the Streak to a sudden end. In those days, it was not unusual for major-league teams to play exhibition games when they didn't have regularly scheduled games. Thus, the Yankees headed for Norfolk, Virginia, on June 29, 1934, to play one of their minor-league teams, the Tars. A huge crowd showed up to

Recently married, and playing some of the best baseball of his career, Gehrig had plenty of reasons to smile as the 1934 season began.

see the superstars from the big city. What they saw was almost a tragic accident.

The game started off well for Gehrig as he hit a home run in the first inning. Unfortunately, in the second inning, pitcher Ray White (another former Columbia student) zinged in a fastball that smacked Gehrig in the forehead. He couldn't get out of the way in time and fell to the ground unconscious. Trainers and teammates rushed to help.

"I swear to God, you would have thought he was dead," said the Tars shortstop, Robert Stevens.

After a few minutes, Gehrig finally came around; fans and players breathed a sigh of relief so big that it was probably felt in New York City. X-rays taken at a nearby hospital showed that his skull was not fractured. He did have a **concussion**, however, and a huge lump over his right eye where the ball had hit.

"I guess the Streak's over now," White said, showing little compassion.

White was wrong, however. The day after, Gehrig played even though he had a lump on his head so large that his regular hat wouldn't fit over it. The team took one of Ruth's and cut some of the seams. Ignoring the pain, Gehrig had three triples in three at bats. However, the game ended before the fifth inning was over because of a rainstorm; Gehrig's efforts didn't count after all.

> "I guess the Streak's over now," White said, showing little compassion.

On July 14, he nearly missed another game. A terrible back pain left him almost unable to walk. However, the Iron Horse dressed for the game and insisted on batting once in order to extend the Streak. McCarthy had him bat first in the order. After Gehrig got a hit and limped to first base, he was taken out for a pinch runner, and another player

Lou Gehrig never missed a game during his years with the Yankees. However, he did have to pull a few fast ones to keep the Streak going. He never denied it, and the Streak is no less an accomplishment, but there were times that he snuck through. He stopped playing early in several games toward the end of those seasons in which the Yankees were far ahead in the standings. In his early years, he was also taken out for pinch hitters on occasion. In addition, he was kicked out of six games for arguing with umpires. One rumor said that Yankees general manager Ed Barrow used a small rainstorm as an excuse to postpone a game for which Gehrig was not well enough to play. Even with those comparatively small issues, Gehrig's Streak is still legendary.

took his place as first baseman when the Yankees took the field. It was a bit of a cheap way to keep his Streak alive.

A Break on the Ocean

While Gehrig continued to dominate the A.L. hitting charts, his partner in power was fading. The 1934 season was the last that the great Babe Ruth would play for the Yankees. As Ruth slowed down, the relationship between Ruth and Gehrig also faded.

Ruth had a surprisingly close relationship with Christina Gehrig, which Lou appreciated as long as Ruth remained respectful. Ruth had grown up without a solid family and seemed to connect with the comfortable home of the Gehrigs. Ruth often visited for dinner, enjoying Mrs. Gehrig's home-cooked meals.

He gave her a Chihuahua dog that she named after one of his nicknames, "Jidge."

Gehrig remained, of course, very loyal and close to his mother. Thus, when he felt that Babe had shown her disrespect, it proved to be damaging to Ruth's and Gehrig's relationship. Babe and his wife Claire visited the Gehrig home with Julia, Claire's daughter, and Dorothy, Babe's daughter that Claire and the Babe were raising together. Mrs. Gehrig didn't approve of Dorothy's tomboyish behavior and style of dress and said something about it to Claire.

Claire became very upset, so Babe said something about it to Lou. Of course, Gehrig defended his mother, no matter what. The harsh words about his mom put another wedge between Lou and Babe.

Finally, the relationship came to an end during a trip in early 1934 to Japan. Now married to Eleanor, Gehrig and his wife joined Ruth and a group of major leaguers headed across the Pacific on an ocean liner to visit Japan and play

Gehrig's mother often traveled to spring training to be with him, as she did here in 1930.

some baseball. On the long boat ride over, the energetic Eleanor found herself hanging out one afternoon with Ruth. The two were alone in his cabin, enjoying drinks and fancy food. Gehrig didn't know where his new wife had gone. Afraid she might have fallen overboard, he had the boat searched. Eleanor didn't turn up until hours later. When Lou learned that she had been hanging out with Babe, he was extremely upset. He did not like his wife spending time with a man he did not respect. A short while later, Babe arrived at their cabin to see Lou. As Eleanor described the scene in her book about her life with Gehrig, the event was the final straw to the relationship between these two great ballplayers. As Ruth came into the cabin, "my unforgiving man turned his back, extending the silent treatment to [Ruth], and Babe retreated. They never did become [friends again], and I just dropped the subject forever."

Lou Gehrig and Babe Ruth will be forever linked thanks to their success with the Yankees and their amazing baseball skills. However, as much as the press tried to create a deep friendship, it most likely didn't exist. Whatever relationship the two men

Lou and Eleanor enjoy a stroll on deck during their cruise to Japan in 1934.

had ended on that ocean liner to Japan. Some people say that the two never talked again. By the end of 1934, Ruth was gone from the Yankees. He was sold to the Boston Braves, who hinted that they would make him a manager—his true dream.

The Gehrigs decided to continue their trip after Japan. This tour with Eleanor was a dream for Lou. The young man who until recently still lived with his mother finally saw the world. They visited countries in Asia, went to India, saw the pyramids in Egypt, and toured Europe. They saw their beloved operas in Rome and enjoyed fabulous food in Paris.

With Ruth gone for the 1935 season, Gehrig cemented his hold on the job of Yankees' leader. "Lou was the perfect team man," outfielder Tommy Henrich said. "He did what he was told and set an example for the rest of us." Therefore, it was not a surprise that his leadership became official in the first year after Ruth left, when Gehrig could finally step out of Ruth's shadow. To kick off the 1935 season, McCarthy named Gehrig as the Yankees' captain on April 12. The team had been without one since 1925, when captain Everett Scott—whose consecutive games streak Lou broke—was traded away from the team.

> . . . his leadership became official in the first year after Ruth left, when Gehrig could finally step out of Ruth's shadow.

Here Comes Joltin' Joe

In 1935, Gehrig was the centerpiece of the team; he was the team captain, and he had another outstanding season. However, the Yankees struggled as a team, finishing behind the Detroit Tigers in the race for the A.L. championship. Impatient to have a hometown champion, New York fans and writers unfairly blamed Gehrig for the team's troubles. Then in 1936, the Yankees welcomed another shining light that would again place Gehrig in a shadow, though one not as deep and wide as Ruth's. A young Italian-American from San Francisco arrived with a sweet swing and a ready-made fan base in immigrant-filled New York City. Joe DiMaggio, known as Joltin' Joe for his powerful bat, came complete with a streak of his own—he had hit in sixty-one straight games for the San Francisco Seals in the Pacific Coast League, the nation's top minor league. He played an outstanding centerfield and had a winning smile and pleasant personality.

DiMaggio proved to be a perfect fit on the already-powerful Yankees. As Gehrig had another stellar year, DiMaggio joined him, Frank Crosetti, and Lefty Gomez to lead the Yankees back to the top of the American League.

DiMaggio also quickly became the most popular player on the team. "He was the biggest star from almost the moment he

Gehrig talks with new teammate Joe DiMaggio at spring training camp in 1936.

Joe DiMaggio (1914–1999)

If anyone could compete with Gehrig for having a great reputation and the lifelong love of the fans, it was Joe DiMaggio. He was known as Joltin' Joe, Joe D., and The Yankee Clipper, after the smooth-sailing old-time ships. DiMaggio played for the Yankees from 1936 to 1951, though he missed the 1943–45 seasons while serving in the army during World War II. During DiMaggio's time with the Yankees, the club won ten pennants and nine World Series. DiMaggio was a three-time MVP. The biggest highlight of his career came in 1941, when he hit in fifty-six straight major-league games. That streak is one of baseball's longest-standing records. No one has come closer than 44 hits in consecutive games since. Following his retirement, DiMaggio was a commercial spokesperson, was married briefly to actress Marilyn Monroe, and was a fixture at Yankees' celebrations. He was introduced for most of his last two decades as "The Greatest Living Ballplayer," though some might say Willie Mays and others had a better claim to that title. DiMaggio was named to the Hall of Fame in 1955 and passed away at age eighty-four in 1999.

hit the Yanks," remembered pitcher Lefty Gomez. "It just seemed a terrible shame for Lou. He didn't seem to care, but maybe he did. They got along together, but how could you ever know how Lou really felt?"

Gehrig, for his part, just kept going and going. He hit .354, had 49 homers (a career high) and 152 RBI, and won his second A.L. Most Valuable Player award that season.

In the 1936 World Series, the Yankees faced the New York Giants, led by ace pitcher Carl Hubbell. "King Carl" knocked off the Yankees in Game 1, but then they came back to win four of the next five games to clinch their first World Series title since 1932. Gehrig had a team-leading 7 RBI in the Series. The Yankees—and Lou Gehrig—were champs again. They wouldn't be anything but, until the next decade.

Another World Series: above is a ticket stub from 1936.

Movie Star Lou

Eleanor, meanwhile, was continuing in her role as Lou's cheerleader. With help from Christy Walsh, she got Lou a tryout as an actor. Inspired by Eleanor's prodding, Gehrig was coming out of his shell a bit. His first try at acting came in late 1936. Lou posed for pictures to audition for the role of Tarzan, King of the Jungle, in a series of movies. However, the producers eventually chose another athlete, Glenn Morris for the role. Morris had won the decathlon—a track and field event—at the Olympics that year.

Eleanor and Lou tried again in the spring, taking a trip to Hollywood for a screen test, which is an audition in front of a camera. Producers signed him to a contract for a cowboy movie called *Rawhide*. He wouldn't be the star, but it was another step out of his quiet life, led by the hand of Eleanor.

In costume for his 1936 film role in *Rawhide*, Gehrig meets one of his co-stars.

The Streak Continues

In the off-season before 1937, Gehrig once again bumped up against Babe Ruth. During discussions for his new contract with club owner Jacob Ruppert, Gehrig read some comments Ruth made in a newspaper article. "I think Lou's making one of the worst mistakes a ballplayer can make by trying to keep up that 'iron man' stuff," Ruth said, referring to the Streak. "He's already cut three years off his baseball life with it. He oughta learn to sit on the bench and rest." In other words, Ruth was saying that Gehrig was hurting himself by playing every day. He believed that if Gehrig let his body rest sometimes, he'd be able to extend his baseball career even longer. For a man who put his love of

While Gehrig was always ready to accept nearly any contract offer that Yankees owner Jacob Ruppert (in suit) offered him, the same was not true of Ruth. The difference was one source of friction between the two players.

his team above just about anything else in his life, this was a real insult. The comments infuriated Gehrig. The man whom he considered a great player but a less-than-great man had, to Gehrig's mind, insulted him. Gehrig was also realistic, however. "If it develops that I'm hurting the team by trying to stay in, I'll get out, and the record will end right there."

During the 1937 season, Gehrig gave Yankees fans no worries about going out there every day. Helped by DiMaggio's amazing bat, the Yankees were again the cream of the American League. Gehrig had 159 RBI, but DiMaggio topped him with 167. Gehrig had a slightly higher average, .351 to .346, but Joltin' Joe had 46 homers to Lou's 37. They made a powerful pair in the Yankees' lineup. The Yankees won the league by thirteen games and then beat the Giants again to win another World Series.

The Yankees had a great year in 1937 and they wrapped up the season with a World Series title. The program from that series is pictured here.

Throughout all this, the Streak went on . . . and on . . . and on. Gehrig started every game from 1934 through 1938. He came out of only a handful of games. Just about any other player would have stopped the Streak much earlier, sitting down with a muscle tear, a cracked finger, a bad cold, or tired legs. However, Gehrig continued to play. (In fact, X-rays taken after he finished his career found seventeen different cracks in the bones of his hands and fingers, cracks he had ignored to keep playing.)

"This 'Iron Man' stuff is bunk," Gehrig stated in May of 1937. "It is true that I have considerable physical strength, but that isn't the answer. There have been many powerful players in baseball who weren't in there every day. It wasn't exceptional strength in my case, nor even exceptional endurance. It was the determination to be in there and to hustle every minute of the time I was there that has made that record a reality." Gehrig had been working toward this streak his whole life—from the time he was a kid, working hard in the gymnasium, working at odd jobs even as he went to school, to watching how hard his mother and others in his neighborhood worked. Gehrig didn't know any other way to approach baseball or life than to work hard every day to be the best he could be.

"It was the determination to be in there and to hustle every minute of the time I was there that has made that record a reality."

As 1938 rolled on toward another championship, Gehrig had one of his worst seasons. He saw his totals drop to their lowest in a decade: 29 homers, 114 RBI, and a .295 batting average. It was the first time he'd been below .300 since 1925. By the middle of that season, fans were even criticizing him for not hitting well. McCarthy dropped him from his usual fourth

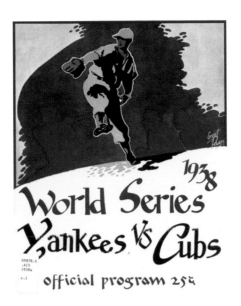

World Series
Yankees vs Cubs

GV878.4
.A15
1938a
c.1

official program 25¢

Though Lou Gehrig had one of his worst years in 1938, the team continued to succeed as it played against the Chicago Cubs in yet another World Series. The 1938 World Series program is shown here.

spot to a lower place in the batting order for a while. Lou started using lighter and lighter bats in order to keep up his swing. In May, Eleanor even suggested that he skip a game and end the Streak in order to rest. "Skip it? You know I can't just skip it," he answered. Gehrig didn't want to admit it to anyone, but things were changing. Lou Gehrig's body was changing, and no one knew why.

CHAPTER 9

The Streak Ends

I watched him run to second base and it looked like he was running uphill.

—*Tommy Henrich*

L ooking back, no one knows for sure when Gehrig actually became sick, but many believe it was in early 1938. He had filmed the movie *Rawhide* then. Doctors and writers since have studied the film carefully to look for early evidence of Gehrig's illness. Others wonder if it was during the 1938 season, when some players saw his bat speed slow down and his timing in the field change. Throughout the off-season before the 1939 schedule, Lou and Eleanor really started noticing that things were not working right with Lou's body. He would fall while ice skating, have trouble with stairs, or experience weakness in his hands.

"One day, he even lost a bout with a ketchup bottle," wrote Eleanor. "He couldn't work the top off, and had to give it to [his Yankees' teammate and friend] Bill Dickey to open."

Eleanor and Lou finally went to see a doctor about Lou's physical problems. He wasn't in pain, but it was obvious that something was wrong. The first doctor thought it was a gallbladder problem. The gallbladder is an organ near the stomach. It helps move fluids around the body, along with the liver. The doctor suggested a new diet, with more fruit, thinking it would help. He was wrong.

By spring training 1939, Gehrig's swing was awkward and teammates were noticing that he was slowing down.

As they watched him during spring training, teammates were also beginning to sense that something was seriously wrong. "In Clearwater one day we played the Phillies," said Tommy Henrich of a spring training game in 1939. "He tried to go from first to third on a hit. I watched him run to second and it looked like he was running uphill. He just wasn't getting anyplace."

"He didn't have a shred of his former power or his timing," wrote Joe DiMaggio in a book years later.

He was awful during spring training games, gathering only a handful of hits and booting many ground balls. From the youngest players to the oldest writers, it was obvious that this was not the Iron Horse they were used to seeing. However, Gehrig played on. "If it isn't good enough, McCarthy will get me out of there," he said. "If it is, then I'll stick." That kind of thinking, though, was just postponing the problem.

The Final Short Season

Gehrig played occasionally during a long string of exhibition games leading to Opening Day, 1939. He didn't do well, however, and often looked terrible.

Gehrig played on, making errors and once even leaving the base paths to avoid the embarrassment of being tagged out for being too slow. On April 30, he played in his 2,130th straight game. He was hitless. The Yankees lost 3–2.

On May 2, 1939, Lou made his decision. He had watched himself miss balls he should have caught and wave at balls he should have hit. A man who had spent a lifetime knowing his body was finally listening to what it was saying. Gehrig met with McCarthy before the game to give him the news—he didn't want to play that day. McCarthy spoke to reporters soon after. "It's a black day for me and the Yankees."

He had watched himself miss balls he should have caught and wave at balls he should have hit.

At the ballpark that day in Detroit, Gehrig took the lineup card out to home plate before the game . . . with his name missing for the first time since 1925. Babe Dahlgren would play first base for the Yankees that day.

"I decided Sunday on this move," he said afterward. "I haven't been a bit of good to the team since the season started. It wouldn't be fair to the boys or to Joe or to the baseball public for me to try going on. In fact, it wouldn't be fair to myself, and I'm the last consideration."

The announcement was made to the fans at the ballpark. "How about a hand for Lou Gehrig, who played 2,130 games in a row before he benched himself today?" said the announcer. As the news spread, the baseball world was shocked.

The Streak was over.

Gehrig watched the game from the dugout. A famous photo taken that day shows him sitting on the dugout steps, watching his teammates on the field. Looking back now, it's a picture of great sadness, a hero taken from his field of glory before his time. Gehrig was only thirty-six years old.

For the next couple of weeks, Gehrig was at almost every game, in uniform. However his duties extended only to walking

This famous photo shows Gehrig sitting on the dugout steps in Detroit watching the first game he had missed playing in since 1925.

Lineup Cards

Before every baseball game, the two teams' managers meet with the umpire and each other. They turn in an official lineup card to the umpires, who use the card to keep track of who is at bat and who has been replaced as the game goes on. The card lists the starting players, the starting pitcher, and the reserve players available for each team. This brief meeting is also used to go over any special rules for the day or for the ballpark.

Lineup cards have become valuable souvenirs. Fans want a record of the players who were part of famous games. The lineup card for the 1933 all-star game, for example, sold in 2007 for $138,000.

slowly out to home plate with the lineup card before every game. It was a sad sight for fans and fellow players to see. There was something seriously wrong with Lou Gehrig—but no one knew exactly just how sick he really was.

The Bad News

On June 13, Lou traveled to Minnesota to visit the Mayo Clinic. The hospital was famous for its ability to figure out illnesses that other hospitals couldn't. It had hundreds of doctors. Patients came from all over, some of them rich and famous like Gehrig. Amazing cures and treatments had been reported at the Mayo Clinic. Gehrig hoped that the experts there could figure out what was wrong with him—and fix it.

Several doctors who were expert at diseases of the nerves examined Gehrig. They asked him endless questions about what

Ever optimistic, Gehrig landed in Minnesota to visit the Mayo Clinic in a search of
what was wrong with him.

he could and could not do. They checked him out from head to
toe. They didn't like what they found.

Lou wrote to Eleanor from Minnesota about what the
doctors found. In typical style, he said that his first concern was
for the health of those around him. He worried that what he
had might be contagious and that he could pass his illness on to
other people by being near them. Lou learned that this was not
true. However, he also wrote, "Playing is out of the question."

He left Minnesota on June 19, 1939, with a letter from the
doctors to Ed Barrow and the Yankees. It contained the bad news.

"Mr. Gehrig is suffering from amyotrophic lateral sclerosis
[ALS]. . . . the nature of this trouble is such that Mr. Gehrig

ALS

Amyotrophic lateral sclerosis [am-ee-oh-TROH-fik LAT-er-ahl skler-OH-sis], known as ALS or "Lou Gehrig's Disease," was first described in 1869 by a French doctor. It is a very rare disease. ALS attacks nerves that control the body's voluntary muscle movement. It remains one of the deadliest and hardest diseases to treat. A person with ALS slowly loses control of all his or her body's functions. However, that person's mind remains sharp and aware. Only about five thousand people each year in the United States are diagnosed with it, out of a population of nearly 300 million. People who have it slowly become completely dependent on others. Eventually, the body simply shuts down. ALS causes a lot of sadness for the family members of patients, too. Millions of dollars are spent each year in trying to find a cure. The exact cause of this disease remains unknown.

will be unable to continue his active participation as a baseball player."

Today, those words are a death sentence. ALS is a fatal disease. There is no cure. At the time, however, ALS was a mystery. Very few doctors and even fewer people had heard of it or understood it. Many people likely thought it was a tough break for Gehrig, but that he would continue to live and be able to pursue other goals, outside of baseball.

Sooner than anyone knew, perhaps sooner than Gehrig himself knew, the sad truth would be evident.

CHAPTER 10

Luckiest Man

I might have been given a bad break, but I've got an awful lot to live for.

By late June 1939, the public was still confused about just what was wrong with Gehrig. Again, not much was known about ALS at the time. The Mayo letter, though, had said that ALS was related to polio, a disease that many people were familiar with back then. Polio could kill a person, but it was seen as more of a disease to possibly live with rather than surely die from. Still, Gehrig's problem was a mystery, and most people assumed that it was something that he would battle and beat, much as he had done with everything that had crossed his path so far.

The movement to honor the stricken star started with a suggestion by sportswriter Paul Gallico. In the past, special "days" had been held to honor retiring players. Speeches were made, gifts presented, and fans were able to say thanks. So to honor Gehrig, the Yankees planned Lou Gehrig Appreciation Day, to be celebrated between the games of a doubleheader on July 4, 1939. The Yankees were playing the Washington Senators.

Behind the scenes, Lou and Eleanor were stunned to learn that general manager Ed Barrow would not keep Gehrig in the Yankees' organization if he indeed could not continue to play. They had assumed that he'd work for the team in some way, but Barrow said he should "start looking for another job." It was a shocking thing to do to someone who had been so intensely loyal for so many years. Barrow never commented on why he wouldn't keep Gehrig onboard.

With Gehrig knowing that his time as a Yankee was ending, but with fans not knowing what the future held for their hero, plans were made for one of baseball's most memorable days. Though he could no longer play the game he loved, Lou Gehrig would put on his pinstriped uniform and have one more shining moment in the sun on the green grass of Yankee Stadium.

The Big Day

On a bright, sunny day, 61,808 fans packed Yankee Stadium for the tribute to Gehrig, an event that would dwarf the two regular games being played that afternoon.

As the first game ended (the Yankees lost 3–2 to the visiting Washington Senators), the two teams gathered on the field, lined up near home plate. Members of the 1927 Yankees also came out onto the field to join them. There was Ruth, Lazzeri, Meusel, Combs, Pennock, Koenig, Hoyt, and others. Wally Pipp, whom Gehrig had replaced long ago, was on the field. Former streak–record-holder Everett Scott came, too.

The speeches began as a representative of each group went to the microphones to praise Gehrig

This ordinary-looking ticket gave a fan admission to a momentous event. Teammates and fans celebrated Lou and bid him farewell at Lou Gehrig Appreciation Day on July 4, 1939.

and give him a gift of some sort. The New York Giants sent a large silver plate. The visiting Senators had a gift—a framed poster that said "Don't Quit." Various Yankees groups, including writers, groundskeepers, employees, and stadium workers, all had something to offer.

New York Mayor Fiorello LaGuardia presented Lou with an award from the city that loved him so. LaGuardia called Gehrig "the best to be found in sportsmanship and citizenship." Babe Ruth spoke. The Postmaster General, representing President Franklin Roosevelt, spoke.

Joe McCarthy told the packed stadium and Lou, "When you told me you were quitting because you felt you were a hindrance to the team . . . My God, man, you were never that!"

Manager Joe McCarthy presents Gehrig with one of several trophies given on Gehrig's "day" at Yankee Stadium.

The master of ceremonies asked if Lou would like to speak, and at first, he shook his head, no . . . no thanks, but then the chant began . . . Lou, Lou, Lou.

"I'd have rather struck out in the ninth with the score tied, two down, and the bases loaded than walk out there before all those grand people," Gehrig said after the event was over. "It's the only time I've ever been frightened on a ball field."

Finally, as the crowd continued to chant, "We want Gehrig!" Lou stepped shyly to the cluster of microphones. He had written a short speech but hoped he would not have to give it. He had practiced the night before anyway and would recite it from memory. He composed himself for a moment. McCarthy stepped over to give him some support, then stepped back. Gehrig looked at the ground, holding his hat in his hand at his

Gehrig pauses at the microphones during his famous "luckiest man" speech on July 4, 1939.

side. He seemed to hesitate again. Then Lou Gehrig stepped up to the plate, as he had so many times in that great baseball landmark. As he had done time and again, he came through in the clutch.

He gave a short speech that included some of the most famous words in American sports history: "Today, I consider myself the luckiest man on the face of the earth."

His speech echoed throughout a vast, silent Yankee Stadium. His head bowed as he spoke the words that, as much as anything he did on the field, would make him a legend. For a man who didn't say much in his life, who guarded his privacy and his feelings carefully, how unexpected that his greatest moment came when he did neither.

After he finished, the fans roared even louder than before. Photographers dashed in to get more pictures. And out of the crowd of people came another legend: Babe Ruth. Ruth was dressed in an all-white linen suit, shining on the field again, casting Gehrig into shadow. In Gehrig's big moment, the big man came over and gave him a big hug. He whispered into his ear. Many people think that they were the first words spoken between the pair for at least five years. It makes a nice story to think the old wounds disappeared there,

It is unclear whether Lou Gehrig and Babe Ruth ever mended their relationship, but Ruth did return to support and honor his old teammate on Lou Gehrig Appreciation Day.

Lou Gehrig's Farewell Speech

Note: Surprisingly, nobody knows exactly what Lou Gehrig said in his famous speech on July 4, 1939. Only four sentences of the speech were preserved on audio recordings: the first two and the last two. The rest of Lou's words survive only in hurriedly transcribed (written down) accounts by journalists in attendance. Different reporters, though, wrote slightly different versions. No two accounts were exactly alike. What follows is one of the many versions.

"Fans, for the past two weeks, you've been reading about the bad break I got. Yet today I consider myself the luckiest man on the face of the earth.

"I've been in ballparks for seventeen years and have never received anything but kindness and encouragement from you fans. Look at these grand men. Which one of you wouldn't consider it the highlight of his career just to associate with him for even one day?

"Sure, I'm lucky. Who wouldn't consider it an honor to have known [Yankees owner] Jacob Ruppert, also the builder of baseball's greatest empire, Ed Barrow. To have spent six years with that wonderful little fellow, Miller Huggins, and to have spent nine more with that outstanding leader, that smart student of psychology, the best manager in baseball today, Joe McCarthy.

"Sure, I'm lucky. When the New York Giants, a team you'd give your right arm to beat and vice-versa, sends you a gift, that's something. When everybody down to the groundskeepers in those white coats remember you with trophies, that's something. When you have a wonderful mother-in-law who takes sides with you and squabbles with her own daughter, that's something. When you have a father and mother who work all their lives so you can have an education and build your body, it's a blessing. When you have a wife who's been a tower of strength and showed more courage than I ever dreamed existed, that's the finest I know.

"So I close in saying that I might have been given a tough break, but I've got an awful lot to live for. Thank you."

A band awaits its cue, the Yankees and the Senators line up, and Mayor LaGuardia speaks during ceremonies on Lou Gehrig Appreciation Day.

but perhaps they really didn't. While many commentators over the years have believed that Ruth and Gehrig ended their feud with that hug, one friend of Gehrig's didn't think it was truly over. "They were never friends again," said Bill Dickey. "You know that famous picture of Babe hugging Lou at the ceremony in 1939? Well, Babe put his arms around Lou and hugged him. But if you look close, Lou never put [both] his arms around the Babe. Lou just never forgave him."

Regardless of that moment, however, Gehrig later told Dickey, "Bill, I'm going to remember this day for a long time."

The ceremony ended, the players retreated to their dugouts, the second game of the doubleheader began, and Lou Gehrig moved off the field for good.

One Big Question

Many wonder if Lou Gehrig knew he was dying as he gave that final speech. There has never been a definitive answer to that question. Eleanor had a lot to do with that, encouraging Lou's doctors to keep information from him on just how serious ALS was. Lou, for his part, seems to have been concerned about keeping Eleanor from worrying. He wrote to his doctors not to tell her about some of the details. He seems not to have reported to her all of what he learned at the Mayo Clinic. Perhaps they each tried to fool the other about how serious the illness was.

Biographer Jonathan Eig discovered a batch of letters to and from Gehrig and his doctors. Eig reports that friends of Gehrig's main doctor, Paul O'Leary, say that the doctor would never have lied to his patients. However, Gehrig's letters make it sound as if he's confident of recovery or even hopeful of a "miracle" cure. He knew he had ALS, but perhaps he didn't truly know, or didn't truly believe, just what having that disease really meant because doctors didn't know much about it at the time. Gehrig certainly could see how his body was deteriorating, and that no matter what he and his doctors tried, he wasn't really getting better. He rode the roller coaster of illness always looking ahead, hoping that the next idea might be the one that cured him. However, that idea never came. Perhaps it was just part of his lifelong positive attitude that he simply wouldn't admit that fatal truth, not to Eleanor, his doctor, or himself. He just couldn't imagine being taken out of the game of life.

> *Gehrig certainly could see how his body was deteriorating, and that no matter what he and his doctors tried, he wasn't really getting better.*

CHAPTER 11

The Final Years

As for myself, it is getting a little more difficult each day, and it will be hard to say how much longer I can carry on.

After his July 4 "day," Gehrig retreated from the spotlight. He watched from the dugout, going to almost every Yankees game—but as a spectator only. The team stormed to another A.L. pennant in 1939, led by DiMaggio's league-leading .381 average, the slugging of outfielder "King Kong" Keller, and Dahlgren's 89 RBI. Then Gehrig watched as the Yankees went on to win a fourth straight World Series, this time over the Cincinnati Reds, and without the Iron Horse to lead them.

As he continued to seek treatments for his disease that fall and winter, Lou did receive some good news. In December, he learned that he had been elected to the National Baseball Hall of Fame, the greatest honor a ballplayer can receive.

But with those honors achieved and no baseball to play, Lou Gehrig had a lot more time on his hands. He spent much of this time as a patient focused on recovering. Doctors were still learning how to treat ALS, and Gehrig was a willing participant in medical experiments. He traveled to the Mayo Clinic to work with doctors there. They held out little hope, but whatever hope they did

The National Baseball Hall of Fame

Located in Cooperstown, a small village in upstate New York, the National Baseball Hall of Fame and Museum opened in 1939. (The Hall of Fame had started electing players in 1936, but the building didn't open until 1939.) The brick buildings there hold thousands of pieces of baseball memorabilia. The Hall also honors those players and others who are selected to be in the Hall of Fame. Players, coaches, managers, umpires, owners, and other team executives are eligible. A group of baseball writers votes each year to choose new members for the Hall. They are inducted, or brought into, the Hall at a popular ceremony each summer. Hundreds of thousands of fans make the long pilgrimage to Cooperstown to visit their heroes' plaques and see the many displays of baseball history. For players, it's the ultimate goal for their careers. For fans, it's the ultimate baseball vacation.

This photograph shows the distinctive red-brick façade of the National Baseball Hall of Fame and Museum. Along with honoring the top players in history, the museum includes thousands of artifacts, 2 million research files, and more than 500,000 black-and-white and color photographs.

offer, Gehrig leaped at like it was a fastball whizzing toward home plate.

"The docs say I may get a break myself," he once told a reporter. "They say there's a fifty-fifty chance that this thing can be checked." We may never know whether Gehrig was just being optimistic or was misinformed about his disease.

Lou Gets a Job

Near the end of the 1939 season, Gehrig received a job offer from New York City Mayor Fiorello LaGuardia. Knowing how well-liked Gehrig was and wanting to help him as well, LaGuardia suggested that Gehrig work for the city's Parole Commission. "I have confidence in you," the mayor said when

New York Mayor Fiorello LaGuardia welcomes Gehrig to his new job as Eleanor looks on.

What Is Parole?

When people are released from jail, they are often placed on what is called parole. That means that while they are free from jail, police officers and judges still want to keep an eye on them. People on parole must check in with parole officers who keep tabs on them. The parole officer's duty is to make sure that people coming out of jail don't fall back into the same bad habits and behaviors that sent them to jail in the first place. Parole officers might help a parolee find a job, an apartment, or counseling. A parole commissioner, such as Gehrig was, helps decide which prisoners should receive parole.

Gehrig suggested that he was not qualified for the job. "All you need is common sense, and you have that." Gehrig took away books and papers and studied late into the summer and as he traveled with the Yankees to Cincinnati for the World Series. In January 1940, he took the job. He was given the files of people who were being released from jail. His job was to help decide when those people would be let out and where they could go once they were.

In the meantime, Lou and Eleanor moved back into New York City (as a city employee, Gehrig was expected to live there). They moved to the Bronx, the same part of the city in which Yankee Stadium was located, into a neighborhood called Riverdale.

Gehrig put as much effort into his new job as he had put into being a ballplayer, or at least as much as his still-weakening body would let him. His constant optimism showed in how he spoke about his job. "I think that many convicted fellows

Unable to play ball, Gehrig kept working, joining the city government as a parole commissioner.

deserve another chance. . . . We don't want anyone in jail who can make good."

However, he couldn't drive anymore due to his failing muscles. Eleanor had to bring him to the office each day. Gehrig had trouble walking to the nearby jails to visit with the people he was helping. He had trouble even signing his name. Through it all, Eleanor was by his side, doing everything she could to make his life easier.

In April 1941, Gehrig requested a six-month leave of absence from the Parole Commission. He told the mayor that he just couldn't keep it up any longer. He would have to leave his job and remain at home.

The End

Throughout 1940 and early 1941, Gehrig continued to hope for a cure or a treatment. He wrote numerous letters to the Mayo Clinic, updating them on how he was doing and asking questions. He tried several experimental treatments in Minnesota and New York, involving various vaccinations and vitamins. However, there was nothing anyone could do. He wrote to one doctor, "As for myself, it is getting a little more difficult each day, and it will be hard to say how much longer I can carry on."

> *". . . it is getting a little more difficult each day, and it will be hard to say how much longer I can carry on."*

By the spring of 1941, ALS had become known in the press as "Lou Gehrig's Disease," a name it still carries today. At that point, Gehrig was unable to do almost anything for himself. Eleanor and nurses had to help him dress, eat, and light his cigarettes. (Lou Gehrig smoked cigarettes and pipes. It was not unusual in those days for people to smoke. The bad effects of smoking were not widely known.)

Teammates, friends, and famous people made the trip to Gehrig's Riverdale home to visit him. They talked baseball or music or about the news of the day. And those who saw him left the house shaking their heads. They knew now, too. The Iron Horse was riding toward the end.

On June 2, 1941, Lou Gehrig, with his wife and his parents by his side, died from the effects of ALS. He was thirty-seven years old.

CHAPTER 12

Lou's Legacy

His life and the way he lived were tribute enough.
—Bill Dickey

The news of Gehrig's death hit baseball hard. Teams held a moment of silence for him at ballparks around the country. Telegrams and flowers arrived by the basketful, addressed to the Yankees or to Eleanor or to Lou's mother. President Franklin Roosevelt was among those who expressed his sorrow at Gehrig's passing. The flags in New York City were lowered in Gehrig's honor.

A few days after his death, Gehrig's body was displayed in its casket at Christ Protestant Episcopal Church in Riverdale. People from all walks of life— kids, adults, ballplayers, and fans—filed by to see their hero one final time. He was buried in Valhalla, New York, about forty-five minutes north of home plate at Yankee Stadium.

A group of young fans—students from Commerce High School—gloves and caps in hands, wait outside a New York City church to see their hero one last time.

On July 4, 1941, Gehrig received another honor from the Yankees. In deep center field, actually on the field of play, the team placed a large granite-and-bronze monument to Gehrig. It sat beside a similar honor placed there in 1932 for Miller Huggins. That pair would be joined by a third for Babe Ruth in 1949. The trio of tombstone-like monuments remained "in play" until 1973, sometimes actually getting in the way of outfielders chasing a ball. During a renovation of Yankee Stadium, the monuments were moved behind the left-field wall. In 2009, this area known as Monument Park was moved to the new Yankee Stadium.

In 1942, the movie *The Pride of the Yankees* was released. Film star Gary Cooper played Gehrig, while Babe Ruth appeared as himself. The plot told the story of Gehrig's life, though with some adjustments to fit the film. Cooper's version of Gehrig as a

Bill Dickey (left) and Joe McCarthy help unveil the monument to Gehrig that joined one for Miller Huggins in the Yankee Stadium outfield. Gehrig's wife, Eleanor, and Mayor LaGuardia look on.

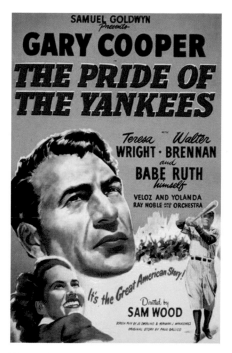

This poster invited fans and moviegoers to see the somewhat fictionalized life of the great Lou Gehrig

solid, stubborn, yet powerful figure remains most people's vision of Gehrig himself. The film covered Gehrig's career with the Yankees, his marriage to Eleanor, his illness, and his memorable speech. (A bit of movie trivia: Cooper was right-handed, so when he batted, he ran to third base. Then the film was flipped over, so it would look like a lefty was running to first.) The sentimental movie remains a classic baseball film.

The Streak Lives Again

Lou Gehrig remains a part of any discussion about the greatest players in history. He roared back to the top of the minds of baseball fans in 1995, as Baltimore Orioles third baseman Cal Ripken, Jr., approached an event that was once thought unthinkable—breaking Gehrig's record streak.

Ripken, like Gehrig, was a top player—though Ripken could never quite match Gehrig's amazing stats. The Baltimore shortstop was an upbeat, hard-working player who did his best every time out. Like Gehrig, he put team first and personal goals second. Still, Ripken's streak was phenomenal. He finally approached Gehrig's magic 2,130 total as 1995 moved on. It was a huge moment for baseball. Only a year earlier, the sport had been hit with a labor problem that forced the first cancellation of the World Series in ninety-one years. Fans were still slowly coming back to their favorite sport when Ripken's quest for the record grabbed the headlines.

On September 6, 1995, facing the Anaheim Angels, Ripken played in his 2,131st consecutive game. He even hit a homer. In the middle of the fifth inning, when the game became official (they did finish and play all nine innings), Ripken took a victory lap amid an ovation that lasted more than fifteen minutes.

Ripken finally decided to sit out a game in 1998, ending the Streak at 2,632 games in a row. Experts say that it's an unreachable goal, but that is what they said about Gehrig's streak, and yet Ripken beat it. He played three more years before retiring in 2001.

A benefit of Ripken accomplishing his amazing feat was a new interest in Gehrig, his great career, and his inspiring story. In 1999, Gehrig earned a well-deserved place on the All-Century Team named by Major League Baseball. He was one of only two first basemen chosen, along with Mark McGwire (whose selection would, looking back, probably not be made today, due to a controversy about McGwire's supposed use of steroids).

The magical number that Cal Ripken, Jr. (at microphone), reached to break Gehrig's "unbreakable" record shows on the wall at Camden Yards in Baltimore.

Other records belonging to Gehrig continue to fall. In 2009, for example, Yankees shortstop Derek Jeter topped Gehrig to become the all-time leader in hits by a Yankees player.

Gehrig does remain, however, fifth on baseball's all-time list with 1,995 RBI. This was the stat that Gehrig cherished more

Baseball's Best Streaks

Here are the top ten consecutive-game streaks in baseball history:

Player	Team	Years	Games
Cal Ripken, Jr.	Baltimore Orioles	1982–98	2,632
Lou Gehrig	New York Yankees	1925–39	2,130
Everett Scott	Boston Red Sox/ New York Yankees	1916–25	1,307
Steve Garvey	Los Angeles Dodgers/ San Diego Padres	1975–83	1,207
Miguel Tejada	Oakland Athletics/ Baltimore Orioles	2000–07	1,152
Billy Williams	Chicago Cubs	1963–70	1,117
Joe Sewell	Cleveland Indians	1922–30	1,103
Stan Musial	St. Louis Cardinals	1952–57	895
Eddie Yost	Washington Senators	1949–55	829
Gus Suhr	Pittsburgh Pirates	1931–37	822

than any other, unsurprisingly, because an RBI helped the team, not himself.

The Fight Goes On

Today, perhaps Gehrig's most lasting **legacy** is in the fight against the disease that took his life and bears his name. In his name, millions of people work to raise money to find a cure. Columbia University's Phi Delta Theta fraternity, of which Gehrig had been a member, created the Lou Gehrig Memorial Award in 1955. A Major League player receives the award each year for character and attitude. The stars that have earned this award include Ozzie Smith, Pete Rose, Don Mattingly (like Gehrig, a Yankees star first baseman), Cal Ripken, Jr., Curt Schilling, George Brett, and John Smoltz. Schilling, an All-Star who last played with the Red Sox in 2008, still serves as a spokesperson for a national organization working to cure ALS. Several ALS organizations also give Lou Gehrig Awards to people who have helped fight for a cure and treatment for "his" disease. In 2009, Gehrig's speech was read aloud at every Major League ballpark as part of a campaign to raise money for ALS research. There is no cure for ALS, but, inspired by Gehrig, many people continue the search.

In that famous speech on July 4, 1939, Gehrig called himself the "luckiest man on the face of the earth." Looking back on his outstanding life, at the courage he showed on and off the field, and his team-first, do-your-best attitude—and the example he set for all of us, fans and nonfans alike—perhaps we are actually the lucky ones who can read about and learn from such a great man.

Glossary

ancestry—people in the past who are related to you.

batting average—a measure of the success of a hitter; it equals the number of hits divided by the number of at bats. A good average is above .300.

batting practice (B.P.)—a period of pregame warm-ups in which players hit easy pitches to get their swings ready for the game to follow.

biographers—people who write about the lives of other people, usually famous people.

bullpen—the area of a ballpark in which pitchers warm up while they wait their turns to come into a game as relief pitchers.

concussion—a condition in which the brain hits against the inside of the skull, usually from a blow or accident.

economic—having to do with money or financial systems.

errors—in baseball, mistakes by fielders that lead to runners on the opposing team reaching base or scoring runs.

fraternity—at colleges, social clubs for young men who pledge to follow secret rules.

grand slam—a home run hit with three runners on base which results in scoring four runs.

immigrants—people who move from the country of their birth to settle in a new country.

legacy—something left behind after a person's death.

major league—the highest level of professional baseball, it is made up of the American and National Leagues. Sometimes called the big leagues.

minor league—in baseball, a group of professional teams at a lower level of skill and budget than the top two major leagues.

motley crew—a group of unrelated people or things that do not seem to belong together.

National Baseball Hall of Fame—located in Cooperstown, New York, it is the place where baseball honors its greatest people. It is also the home of a treasure trove of memorabilia.

newsreels—short films that included information about the events of the day from the 1930s to the 1950s. They were shown before longer feature movies.

pennants—in baseball, the term for league championships. When a team won its league championship, it "won the pennant," because of the triangle-shaped flag that was awarded to the winning team.

pinch hitter—a substitute player who bats in place of another during a game.

promoter—a person who organizes and often pays for an event.

punter—a football player that kicks the football on fourth down.

rookies—players in their first year of pro sports.

rosters—the lists of players on sports teams.

running back—in football, an offensive player that carries the football or catches passes.

runs batted in (RBI)—a statistic that counts when a player causes another player to score a run. A player can also gain an RBI by hitting a home run. Having 100 RBI or more in a season is a very good year for any batter.

semipro—a level of sports in which players are paid a little but not enough to live on comfortably.

stock market—the system that gives people a way to buy and sell parts, or shares, of companies.

wild pitch—when a pitcher throws the ball in such a way that the catcher cannot catch it.

Bibliography

Books

Bak, Richard. *Lou Gehrig: An American Classic*. Dallas: Taylor Publishing, 1995.

Barra, Allen. *Clearing the Bases: The Greatest Baseball Debates of the Last Century*. New York: Thomas Dunne Books, 2002.

Creamer, Robert. *Babe: The Legend Comes to Life*. New York: Simon and Schuster, 1974.

Eig, Jonathan. *Luckiest Man: The Life and Death of Lou Gehrig*. New York: Simon & Schuster, 2005.

Einstein, Charles, ed. *The Baseball Reader*. New York: Lippincott and Crowell, 1956.

Gallico, Paul. *Lou Gehrig: Pride of the Yankees*. New York: Grosset & Dunlap, 1942.

Gehrig, Eleanor, and Joseph Durso. *My Luke and I*. New York: Thomas Crowell, 1976.

Pietrusza, David, Matthew Silverman, and Michael Gershman, eds. *Baseball: The Biographical Encyclopedia*. New York: Total/Sports Illustrated, 2000.

Ritter, Lawrence S. *The Glory of Their Times*. New York: William Morrow, 1966.

Robinson, Ray. *Iron Horse: Lou Gehrig in His Time*. New York: W.W. Norton & Co., 1990.

Web Sites

Newman, Mark. "Gehrig's Shining Legacy of Courage," MLB.com, June 18, 2003. http://newyork.yankees.mlb.com/nyy/history/gehrig.jsp.

"The Official Site of Lou Gehrig." www.lougehrig.com.

Schwartz, Larry. "Gehrig Legacy One of Irony," ESPN.com, 2007. www.espn.go.com/sportscentury/features/00014204.html.

Source Notes

The following citations list the sources of quoted material in this book. The first and last few words of each quotation are cited and followed by their source. Complete information on referenced sources can be found in the Bibliography.

Abbreviations:
BABE—*Babe: The Legend Comes to Life*
CTB—*Clearing the Bases: The Greatest Baseball Debates of the Last Century*
GLI—"Gehrig Legacy One of Irony"
GSL—"Gehrig's Shining Legacy of Courage"
IH—*Iron Horse: Lou Gehrig in His Time*
LG—www.lougehrig.com
LGAC—*Lou Gehrig: An American Classic*
LGP—*Lou Gehrig: Pride of the Yankees*
LM—*Luckiest Man: The Life and Death of Lou Gehrig*
ML—*My Luke and I*

Image Credits

AP Images: 46, 74, 101, 105, 107, 110, 113

Courtesy of James Buckley, Jr.: 111

© Bettmann/CORBIS: 4, 8, 22, 23, 33, 40, 57, 58, 61, 67, 72, 78, 81, 83 (bottom), 89, 93, 97, 98, 99, 109

© H. Armstrong Roberts/ClassicStock/CORBIS: 68

© Rudy Sulgan/CORBIS: 19

© Underwood & Underwood/CORBIS: 39, 63, 73, 79

Getty Images: 53

Library of Congress: 5, 6, 10

National Baseball Hall of Fame Library, Cooperstown, NY: 9, 12, 13, 15, 20, 21, 27, 28, 29, 31, 34, 38, 42, 43, 48 (left and right), 54, 55, 56, 60, 62, 64 (top and bottom), 75, 83 (top), 85, 87, 96, 104

Photo by Joe Robbins: 17

Mark Rucker/Transcendental Graphics: 25, 36, 44, 45, 50, 70, 84, 91

Cover art: MLB Photos via Getty Images

About the Author

James Buckley, Jr., is one of America's leading sports authors for young readers, with more than fifty books to his credit. They include biographies of Péle, Muhammad Ali, Venus and Serena Williams, Bill Bradley, and Roberto Clemente. Baseball is his specialty, and his books on the sport include *Eyewitness Baseball, The Visual Dictionary of Baseball, Baseball: A Celebration, Play Ball: The Official Major League Guide for Young Players*, and *Obsessed with Baseball* (co-author). He is also the author or co-author of the popular *Scholastic Books of Lists 1 and 2* and *Scholastic Book of Firsts*. A member of the Society for American Baseball Research, he has worked for *Sports Illustrated* and NFL Publishing. He is currently the president of the Shoreline Publishing Group, a book producer in Santa Barbara, California; and he is on the board of directors of the Santa Barbara Foresters, a two-time national championship summer-league baseball team (for whom he has also done radio play-by-play).

Index